That Was Halloween
Essays on the Holiday
by
Terence Towles Canote

ISBN-13: 978-1977635365
ISBN-10: 1977635369

Contents

Foreword

I have celebrated Halloween nearly as long as I can remember. One of my earliest memories is going to a Halloween party with my parents and my brother when I was only four years old. It was in our community's old school house, which was decked out with Halloween decorations. I don't remember much about the various activities at the party, although I know apple bobbing was among them.

I can't remember when I first went trick-or-treating, but I know it must have been when I was very young. I grew up on a farm where the neighbours might live some distance away, so my parents always took my brother and me trick-or-treating. We always went to our various relatives' and family friends' houses. I always suspected that the kids who lived in town visited more houses than we did, but then we were not hurting when it came to candy. It would take us literally days to go through it all.

I am fairly certain that my experience of Halloween when I was growing up varies only a little from other Americans who were born in the latter half of the 20th Century. By the time I was born Halloween was already a well-established tradition in the United States, celebrated by millions of Americans. It was also already very commercialised, with a wide array of Halloween merchandise to be bought from September through October. After the winter holidays it is the second favourite holiday of many Americans. I include myself in that number, Halloween being second only to the Yuletide as my favourite holiday.

This admittedly short book is a collection of essays dedicated to Halloween. In these essays I touch upon the evolution of the holiday, its various traditions, and even its portrayal in the movies and on television. My goal for this book is not simply to educate people about the history of Halloween, but to also bring back fond memories for those who have always celebrated the holiday.

Happy Halloween!

Terence Towles Canote
September 2017

An Overview of Halloween

All Saints' Day

According to a 2015 Harris Poll, Halloween is the third favourite holiday of Americans, after Christmas and Thanksgiving. And while the money Americans spend at Halloween is dwarfed by many other holidays (including Easter, Valentine's Day, Mother's Day, and Father's Day), it is still a considerable amount. In 2015 American spent $6.9 billion on Halloween. $2.5 billion of that was on costumes and $2.1 billion was spent on candy. While for many years the secular celebration of Halloween was limited to North America, it has since spread elsewhere in the English speaking world. In the United Kingdom £310 million was spent on Halloween in 2015.

While many of the traditions associated with the modern day celebration of Halloween developed recently, the holiday itself is rather old. Strictly speaking, Halloween is the eve of All Hallows' Day, better known in modern English as All Saints' Day. It was early in the development of Christianity that the church began honouring martyrs on the dates they died. Over the centuries the number of individual martyrs grew so great that a feast day could not be assigned to each and every one. All Saints' Day then developed as a means of honouring all martyrs.

Days commemorating all saints were not unknown before the establishment of All Saint's Day. In the early 4th Century the church in Antioch observed a day for all of the martyrs on the Sunday after Pentecost. It was also in the 4th Century St. Ephrem the Syrian wrote of a feast for all saints observed by the church in Edessa on May 13. In the 5th Century St. John Chrysostom mentioned that the church in Constantinople observed a common day for saints on the Sunday after Pentecost. It was in 609 CE that Pope Boniface IV consecrated the Basilica of St. Mary of the Angels and the Martyrs on May 13. The anniversary of the dedication of the Basilica of St. Mary of the Angels and the Martyrs would continue to be observed in Rome, as well as in many other parts of Europe and Asia.

While the anniversary of the dedication of the Basilica of St. Mary of the Angels and the Martyrs would serve as a common day for martyrs throughout much of the early church, the dates of common days for all the martyrs would vary from place to place for years. Many churches in the East continued to observe the Sunday after Pentecost as a feast day for all the martyrs. According to Saint Óengus of Tallaght, in the 7th and 8th Centuries the church in Ireland celebrated All Saints' Day on April 20. Churches in England and Germany were already observing All Saints' Day on November 1 by the beginning of the 8th Century if the *Homiliae Subdititiae*, falsely ascribed to Bede, is to be believed. It was in the mid-eighth century that Pope Gregory III established November 1 officially as All Saints' Day.

Pagan Autumn Festivals

The date of November 1 coincided with a Celtic festival that marked the end of the harvest season and the beginning of winter. Among the Cornish Kalan Gwav was the first day of winter. Its eve, Nos Kalan Gwav (October 31), in historical times was observed as St. Allan's Day or Allantide. The Irish, Manx, and Scots also had a festival on November 1, called in Modern Irish *Samhain*, in Scottish Gaelic *Samhainn*, and in Manx *Sauin*. In Wales November 1 was observed as Calan Gaeaf, the first day of winter.

Very little is known for certain as to how ancient pagan Celts might have celebrated these festivals, although Irish mythology provides us with some hints. The myth *Serglige Con Culainn* ("Cúchulainn's Sickbed") tells how a festival held by the Ulaid lasted three days before Samhain and three days after (which including Samhain itself would be a full seven days). There were games, assemblies, and feasts. The story *Macgnímartha Finn* ("The Boyhood Deeds of Fionn) states the sídhe (the mounds that were home to the Aos Sí, a supernatural race comparable to the elves of the Germanic peoples or the modern day conception of fairies) were always open on Samhain. The *Lebor Gabála Érenn* ("Book of Invasions") suggests sacrifices may have taken place at Samhain. Every Samhain the folk of Nemed had to give two thirds of their children, grain, and milk to the Formorians (a supernatural, giant race). Both the *Dindsenchas* and the *Annála Ríoghachta Éireann* ("Annals of the Four Masters") claim that a first born child would be sacrificed to the god Crom Cruach in Magh Slécht.

While November 1 was the date of festivals celebrated by the various Celtic peoples, it does not explain why the English and Germans celebrated All Saints' Day on November 1 or why Pope Gregory chose November 1 as its official date. That having been said, some of the Germanic peoples had a festival that fell in October and it seems possible some of the other Germanic peoples might have celebrated a festival around that time as well. Icelandic sources attest *vetrnætr* (literally "Winter Nights"), which *An Icelandic-English Dictionary* by Richard Cleasby and Gudbrand Vigfusson defines as "the three days which begin the winter season." Such sources as the *Fornmanna Sögur* and *Gísla saga Súrssonar* attest that sacrifices took place at Winter Nights. Feasting also took place over the three days of Winter Nights, as shown by *Eyrbyggja Saga* and *Gísla saga Súrssonar*. The dates during which Winter Nights were celebrated varied a bit from year to year. According to our modern calendar, the festival would have roughly taken place in mid-October.

It seems possible that, like the Old Norse speakers, other Germanic peoples also celebrated the beginning of winter. In his treatise *De temporum ratione*, Bede mentions that the Angles and Saxons in England called the month when winter began *Winterfylleþ*, which he interpreted as "winter full moon", because winter began on the full moon of that month. According to Bede, Winterfylleþ was followed by a month called *Blótmónaþ*, literally "sacrifice month." He states that it was the month during which cattle to be slaughtered were dedicated to the gods. The *Menologium seu Calendarium Poeticum*, an Old English poem about the months, equates *Blótmónaþ* with November. Given the Angles and Saxons also thought of winter as beginning in autumn and apparently made sacrifices during that period too, it seems possible that they might have celebrated the beginning of winter much as the Old Norse speakers did.

Given the Angles and Saxons originated on the Continent, it would seem likely that the Germanic peoples there would have also thought of winter as beginning in autumn. Unfortunately, there appears to be no Continental equivalent to Winterfylleþ, although they appear to have a month name that was equivalent to Blótmónaþ. Early modern Dutch attests an alternative name for November, *Slachtmaand*, literally "slaughter month". This alternative name for November is also seen in West Frisian, *Slachtmoanne*, again literally "slaughter month". While both month names may simply reference the fact that cattle were slaughtered in November, it also seems possible that they contain memories of when cattle were also sacrificed to the gods, much as the Angles and Saxons in England did.

Of course, beyond Bede's statement that the Angles and Saxons regarded Winter as beginning during the full moon of Winterfylleþ, we have no clear cut dates as to when they might have celebrated the beginning of winter or made sacrifices. Given the fact that England (and the Continent, for that matter) tends to be a warmer climate than Iceland and Scandinavia, it seems possible that they might have regarded winter as beginning a little bit later than the Old Norse speakers. This could go a long way to explaining why churches in England and Germany chose to celebrate

All Saints' Day on November 1. It would place the Christian festival close to a pagan festival once celebrated in England. It could also explain why Pope Gregory chose November 1 as the official date for All Saints' Day. It would seem to make more sense than Pope Gregory having chosen the date because of Samhain. Indeed, as pointed out above, prior to Pope Gregory making November 1 the official date, All Saints' Day was celebrated on April 20 in Ireland.

While the Celtic peoples celebrated a festival around the time of what would be All Saints' Day and it seems likely that Angles and Saxons in England did as well, it is difficult to say how much impact any of these festivals might have had on later celebrations of Halloween. Certainly the idea of Halloween as a time when the boundaries between worlds became more flexible could stem from the Celtic festival variously called Samhain, Kalan Gwav, and so on. As mentioned above, the Irish apparently believed the mounds of the Aos Sí were open on Samhain. It seems possible that the Angles and Saxons may have held similar beliefs about the beginning of winter, although there is little to suggest this. Regardless, many of the customs we observe at Halloween today are not attested until much later. For example, as much as many would like to trace trick or treating back to earlier traditions, from all appearances it is a modern day development. Regardless, it seems likely that the fact that pagan festivals were celebrated in the British Isles and on the Continent around November 1 were much of what led Pope Gregory to set that as the official date of All Saints' Day.

All Souls' Day

While whether some degree of continuity exists between various pre-Christian holidays and Halloween is debatable, it seems clear that the modern day, secular celebration of Halloween was influenced to some degree by traditions associated with All Souls' Day. For those of you who may be unfamiliar with All Souls' Day, it is a Christian holiday remembering all Christians who have died. It is celebrated on November 2. Alongside Halloween (All Saints' Eve) and All Saints' Day, it is part of Allhallowtide.

Prayers for the dead were established as a tradition very early in the history of Christianity. As early as the 3d Century CE, Roman Christians offered up prayers for the dead in the catacombs. In the 6th Century CE, Pope Gregory offered masses for the souls in Purgatory. It was also in the 6th Century that Benedictine monasteries set aside a day each year to pray for their members who had died and gone to Purgatory. In the 7th Century CE in Spain the first Saturday following Pentecost was set aside for praying for the dead. It was in the 10th Century in Germany that October 1 was established as a common day for praying for the dead. It was Saint Odilo of Cluny who established November 2 as the day for commemorating the dead at the Abbey of Cluny and those monasteries connected to it. The date of November 2 for All Souls' Day was adopted by other Benedictine monasteries and then spread to churches throughout Europe.

Over time All Souls' Day would develop its own traditions. One common to most countries in Europe were the ringing of bells in memory of the dead. In the book *British Popular Customs, Present and Past: Illustrating the Social and Domestic Manners of the People: Arranged According to the Calendar of the Year* by Thomas Firminger and Thiselton Dyer, it mentions a custom in Wexford, Ireland, whereby a candle would be placed in every window of a house on the night of All Souls' Day.

Perhaps the best known custom associated with All Souls' Day was that of "souling". Souling was a tradition whereby children would go from house to house asking for "soul cakes" in exchange for prayers for the dead. Soul cakes were generally made of sweet spices such as allspice, cinnamon, ginger, nutmeg, and so on. The custom is attested fairly early. In his *Book of Festivals*, also known as *Festial*, John Mirk wrote "...wherefore in olden time good men and women would this day buy bread and deal it for the souls they loved, hoping each loaf to get a soul out of purgatory." *Festial* dates to the 1380s. It is also referenced in William Shakespeare's *Two Gentleman of Verona*, Act II, Scene I, "..to speak puling, like a beggar at Hallowmas." Here one might be tempted to see souling as the direct ancestor of modern day trick or treating, but there seems to be no link between the two. A direct line cannot be traced from souling in medieval Britain to trick or treating in 20th Century North America.

Over time the traditions of All Souls' Day would become conflated with those of Halloween and All Saints' Day. In John Aubrey's *Miscellanies*, published in 1714, he tells how soul cakes were heaped upon each other on All Hallows Eve and how every visitor was expected to take one. In *Curiosities of Popular Customs ... Illustrated* by William Shepard Walsh, published in 1897, told how in Ripon, Yorkshire Halloween was known as "Cake Night" and women there would make a cake for every member of their families. Indeed, in *Two Gentelman of Verona*, Shakespeare speaks of "a beggar at Hallowmas", rather than "a beggar at All Souls' Day."

The conflation of "All Souls' Day" with "All Saints' Day" and its eve would have an impact on the development on Halloween. If Halloween wasn't already a night for the dead, it would have eventually become one.

Early Halloween Traditions

While Pope Gregory I set November 1 as the date of All Saints' Day in the 8th Century CE, it is not until much later that many customs connected to Halloween are attested. In fact, our word *Halloween* is actually of rather recent vintage. *Halloween* can ultimately be traced back to the word *All Hallows' Eve* (also rendered *All Hallows' Even*). *All Hallows Eve* itself did not appear in print until about 1556. In Scottish English *All Hallows Even* would eventually be abbreviated to *All Hallowe'en*. By about 1745 *All Hallowe'en* would become simply *Hallowe'en*. Of course, since then the word has lost the apostrophe.

Regardless, among the earliest customs mentioned with regards to *Halloween* is the ringing of bells throughout Allhallowtide. In a sermon at Blanford Forum in 1570, William Kethe mentioned that

"...there was a custom, in the Papal times, to ring bells at Allhallow-tide for all Christian souls." During the reign of Queen Elizabeth I an injunction was actually made against the "...superfluous ringing of bells at Allhallowtide and at All Souls' Day, with the two nights next before and after..."

Bonfires were another early custom mentioned with regards to Halloween. Of course, in Northern Europe bonfires had a long association with various holidays. The Third Council of Constantinople in 680 CE actually attempted to ban bonfires, "Those fires that are kindled by certain people on new moons before their shops and houses, over which also they use ridiculously and foolishly to leap, by a certain ancient custom...." The Third Council of Constantinople was apparently not successful, as bonfires continued to be lit at such holidays as May Day and Midsummer (St. John's Day). Indeed, among the expenses listed of King Henry VII of England were those for making the bonfire for Midsummer Eve.

Just as bonfires were lit on May Day and Midsummer Eve in England, so too were bonfires lit on Halloween in Scotland. In 1772 Welsh naturalist and antiquarian Thomas Pennant wrote of the people of Maylin, near Pitlochrie in Scotland, "Hallow Eve is also kept sacred; as soon as it is dark, a person sets fire to a bush of broom fastened round a pole, and, attended with a crowd, runs about the village. He then flings it down, heaps great quantity of combustible matters on it, and makes a great bonfire." It is notable that Robert Burns's famous poem "Halloween" (which dates to 1785) is filled with fiery imagery.

While bells and bonfires at Halloween have more or less fallen by the wayside, the wearing of costumes at Halloween is a custom that continues to be popular. At least from 16th Century Scotland there was the custom of guising, whereby young men would go in disguise from house to house singing songs or reciting verses in exchange for gifts of food. While the custom sounds like it could be the direct ancestor of trick or treating, it must be stressed that there is no direct link between the two customs.

Another custom that would persist into modern times is that of Halloween pranks. One of the earliest references to pranks being pulled at Halloween occurs in John Mayne's poem "Halloween" (published in 1780), "What fearfu' pranks ensue!" In his *Etymological Dictionary of the Scottish Language* (published in 1808) under the entry for "Candle and Castock" Scottish antiquarian John Jamieson describes a turnip lantern (essentially an early jack o' lantern--more in a little bit) that was used by youngsters to frighten people on Halloween.

Divination would also be a Halloween custom that would survive into modern times. Indeed, in his poem "Halloween" Robert Burns described how single young people went out hand in hand into the cabbage patch to pull the first stalk they saw. The size and shape of the stalk was thought to be indicative of what his or her future spouse would look like. Although most people today probably do not think of Halloween as a particularly romantic holiday, much of the divination practised on Halloween tended to deal with marriage.

While many of Halloween's customs can be traced back to the 17th and 18th Centuries, the carving of jack o' lanterns in connection with the holiday would seem to be of more recent vintage. While the use of vegetables to make lanterns goes back a few centuries, they would not be called "jack o' lanterns" for some time, nor would they be identified with Halloween for some time either. References to such lanterns as part of a Halloween celebration would not appear in print until John Jamieson's *Etymological Dictionary of the Scottish Dictionary* under his above cited entry for "Candle and Castock" in 1808. The first reference of such lanterns as "jack o' lanterns" would not appear in print until a few years later, in Samuel Taylor Coleridge's review of Charles Maturin's play *Bertram* in 1817.

While various traditions associated with Halloween appear to be of relatively recent vintage, the idea of Halloween as a time when the dead and other supernatural entities walk the earth appears to go back many centuries. While there seems to be little evidence for very much continuity between the Irish festival of Samhain and the modern holiday of Halloween, as mentioned earlier in the story *Macgnímartha Finn* ("The Boyhood Deeds of Fionn) it said that the sídhe (the mounds that were home to the Aos Sí) were always open on Samhain. As to Halloween itself, the traditional ballad "Tam Lin" is set at Halloween and deals with the rescue of Tam Lin from the Queen of the Fairies. It is believed to date back in some form to 1549. The traditional ballad "Allison Gross", about the efforts of the ugliest witch in the north county to win a man's heart, also references Halloween. It is believed to date to 1800. It should come as no surprise that one of the most famous early works about Halloween reference the supernatural. John Mayne's poem "Halloween" makes reference to bogles, fairies, and witches.

Halloween Comes to America

By the end of the 18th Century in Scotland Halloween was a well-established holiday to which was attached a number of customs. This was not the case with the British Colonies in North America. While All Saints' Day was recognised as a holy day by Anglicans and Catholics living in the Colonies, Halloween itself was not widely observed. This would remain true in the United States in the late 18th and early 19th Centuries. In fact, for much of the 19th Century when American newspapers mention Halloween at all, it is as a peculiarly Scottish holiday.

This would begin to change when Scots began to immigrate en masse to the United States in the 19th Century. The year 1846 saw the beginning of the Highland Potato Famine, during which time potato crops in Scotland were destroyed by potato blight year after year. Ultimately the Highland Potato Famine would last around ten years, finally coming to an end in 1856. During this period many Highlanders moved from the Scottish Highlands. Some simply moved to the Scottish Lowlands. Others would immigrate to Australia, Canada, and even the United States.

Quite naturally, the Scots brought their Halloween celebrations with them. Initially celebrated only among Scottish and Irish communities in the United States, the celebration of Halloween eventually spread throughout American society. By the 1880s many Americans were holding Halloween parties. For instance, under the "City News" section of the November 1 1883 issue of the *Logansport Pharos Tribune* from Logansport, Indiana, it is mentioned that, "Miss Emma Rosentbail held a very pleasant Halloween party at her home last evening." By the 1890s Halloween parties had become so commonplace throughout the United States that issues of some newspapers might contain references to multiple parties. The November 1 1891 issue of the *Helena Independent* from Helena, Montana mentioned no less than five separate Halloween parties held in the area.

While Halloween parties were a welcome way for Americans to celebrate the holiday in the late 19th Century, a less welcome custom brought over from Scotland was that of Halloween pranks. The November 5 1895 issue of *The Semi-Weekly Cedar Falls Gazette* from Cedar Falls, Iowa mentions an odd prank by some boys in which they tied a light wagon behind the Burlington Passenger No. 5. The train was a half hour late as a result of the prank. The October 31 1893 issue of *The Bloomington Leader* from Bloomington, Illinois mentions that the previous year Halloween pranks had cost the town $800.

Sally Benson tells of a rather odd prank in her semi-autobiographical vignette "October, 1903" (one of the vignettes in her series *5135 Kensington*), first published in the November 1 1941 issue of *The New Yorker* and included in the 1942 book *Meet in St. Louis*. Quite simply, individuals would be hit with flour and then said to be "killed". This custom would later be portrayed in the musical based on the book, *Meet Me in St. Louis* (1944).

By the 1900s Halloween was so widely celebrated in the United States that Halloween merchandise became available. The 1900s saw the first Halloween cards printed. The decade also saw the emergence of paper Halloween decorations. Many of these paper decorations were manufactured in Germany during the decade, although American companies would soon jump on the Halloween bandwagon. The Dennison Manufacturing Company began manufacturing paper Halloween decorations in the 1900s. Their Halloween decorations were so popular that in 1909 Dennison printed its first *Dennison's Bogie Book for Halloween*, which was a guide for decorating for the holiday. Another edition of *The Dennison's Bogie Book* was published in 1912. Except for the years of World War I, it would be published annually until 1934. Another American company well known for their paper Halloween decorations is the Beistle Company. Founded in 1900, the Beistie Company started making Halloween decorations in 1920. The Beistle Company continues to manufacture paper Halloween decorations to this day.

It was in the 1920s that a new custom emerged that is now so strongly associated with Halloween that it is difficult to picture a time when it wasn't practised on the holiday. Trick-or-treating is a custom whereby children in costume go from house to house asking for treats with the phrase, "Trick-or-treat". The implication of the phrase is that if the children are not given treats, then they will play a trick (a Halloween prank) on the residents of the house. Trick-or-treating resembles such earlier customs as souling on All Souls' Day in England and guising on Halloween in Scotland, but trick-or-treating appears to have no direct link to either of them. It appears to have entirely developed in the 20th Century.

Indeed, the first known appearance of the phrase "trick-or-treat" in print is in the November 4 1927 issue of the *Herald* (published in Lethbridge, Alberta) in the article "'Trick or Treat' is the Demand". From Alberta, Canada the custom of trick-or-treating apparently spread to parts of the American Northwest and West, as evidenced by articles on the custom in 1934 in newspapers in Portland, Oregon and Helena, Montana. As the Thirties progressed, trick-or-treating made its way east. A story on trick-or-treating appeared in the October 31 1938 issue of *The Hammond Times* in Indiana. By the early Forties trick-or-treating had reached the East Coast. There was an article on it in the October 24 1942 issue of *The Cumberland Evening Times* in Maryland.

It is difficult to say precisely how the custom of trick-or-treating came about, but it seems likely it emerged from the custom of Halloween pranks. At some point in the Twenties some youngsters in Canada, perhaps observing the shakedown techniques of the gangsters of the era, realised they could get treats by threatening tricks if they did not get them. Quite naturally, such a custom would prove popular with children and so it spread from Canada into the United States. It is notable that many of the early articles on trick-or-treating are somewhat negative in tone, many of them treating it as a form of extortion. As time passed, many articles began to appear that were much more sympathetic in tone to trick-or-treating. Quite simply, as trick-or-treating grew in popularity, there was also a decrease in the number of pranks on Halloween. Over the course of the 20th Century Halloween pranks would decrease to the point that they were relatively rare.

Of course, in order for children to trick-or-treat, they must have costumes to wear. In the late 19th Century and early 20th Century nearly all Halloween costumes were home-made. As the 20th Century progressed, various companies would begin manufacturing costumes for Halloween. It was in the 1920s that Collegeville Flag and Manufacturing Company, a company that originally made flags, began making Halloween costumes commercially available. The J. Halpern Company, later known as Halco, also entered the Halloween costume market. Perhaps the best known name in Halloween costumes in the 20th Century was Ben Cooper, Inc., which began making Halloween costumes in 1937. Collegeville, Halco, and Ben Cooper would dominate the Halloween costume market for the better part of the 20th Century.

In fact, Collegeville, Halco, and Ben Cooper would partly be responsible for a shift in Halloween costumes over the course of the 20th Century. In the late 19th Century and early 20th Century, most costumes tended to be spooky in nature, with people dressing up as ghosts, witches, and devils, with policemen, firemen, and clowns (the non-scary kind) being the exception to the rule. It was in the Thirties that companies began manufacturing costumes of licensed characters. From 1935 to 1938 Halco manufactured costumes based on the characters from *Thimble Theatre*, including Popeye, Olive Oyl, and Wimpy. In the late Thirties Collegeville put out a Lone Ranger costume. Ben Cooper held the licenses to make costumes of the various Walt Disney characters (including Snow White from the blockbuster movie *Snow White and the Seven Dwarfs*). Following World War II, the licensing of characters would begin to play a bigger and bigger role in the production of commercial Halloween costumes, to the point that the majority of costumes made by Ben Cooper and Collegeville were characters from movies, TV shows, and comic books.

While children in the post-war era might elect to dress as Hopalong Cassidy or Batman rather than a ghost or goblin, Halloween has never entirely lost its association with the supernatural. From the early days one has to suspect that many individuals elected to visit houses believed to be haunted on Halloween. The 20th Century saw the emergence of what are called "haunted attractions", which try to simulate the experience of going through a haunted house. The first such haunted attraction was the Orton and Spooner Ghost House in Liphook, East Hampshire. It opened in 1915.

Haunted attractions that were open only during the season of Halloween began to emerge in the United States in the 1930s. An article on a Halloween party from the November 2 issue of the *Kingsville Record* in Kingsville, Texas mentions that "...the youngsters were taken through the haunted house by the Halloween witch." That having been said, haunted attractions would not really take off until the 1950s. The late Fifties saw several such attractions open in California, including the San Mateo Haunted House in 1957 (sponsored by the Children's Health Home Junior Auxiliary) and the San Bernardino Assistance League Haunted House in 1958. The Sixties saw several haunted attractions open across the country, including the Children's Museum Haunted House in Indianapolis. First opened in 1964, it has become the longest running "haunted house" in the United States. Such haunted attractions open during the Halloween season are often fundraisers for various organisations, such as the Jaycees, the March of Dimes, and so on.

By the 1950s Halloween was already a very popular holiday in the United States. It was also highly commercialised. In addition to the paper Halloween decorations and commercially produced Halloween costumes that had been produced for years, the Fifties saw Halloween goods made from plastic emerge. It was during the Sixties that blown mould plastic lawn ornaments, including several dedicated to Halloween, peaked in popularity. Plastic, Halloween merchandise from candy containers to flash lights continue to be made to this day.

Since then Halloween has grown in popularity to where it is the third most popular holiday in the United States. That is not to say that the holiday has not continued to change and evolve. Sometime in the mid-Nineties a new variation on trick-or-treating emerged. Trunk-or-treat is a community event whereby children go trick-or-treating from car to car in a parking lot (usually one belong to a school, city hall, church, or other community building). Precisely where trunk-or-treat first started, much less how it came about, is not known. That having been said, it would explode in popularity in 2006 and has grown in popularity ever since. It seems to be a particularly attractive alternative to traditional trick-or-treating for churches that see Halloween as a "pagan" festival and trick-or-treating with it (at such churches children are encouraged to dress as characters from the Bible).

Afterword

To degree the origins of Halloween are shrouded in mystery. Both the Celtic and Germanic peoples had pagan festivals around the same date, but it is difficult to say that they had much in the way of continuity with Halloween. It is unclear when or why many of the customs now associated with Halloween emerged. What we do know is that it was a particularly popular holiday in Scotland and that Scots immigrating to the United States brought it to North America. Since that time it has grown in popularity and is even growing in popularity elsewhere in the world. It is difficult to say how Halloween may evolve in the future, but one thing seems certain. It will most certainly continue to be a very popular holiday.

Jack o' Lanterns

The jack o' lantern is one of the many symbols associated with Halloween. What is more, unlike ghosts, witches, black cats, and so on, it would seem to be exclusively associated with that holiday. Precisely how pumpkins carved with faces became linked to Halloween is unclear. Many books and web sites have detailed explanations of how jack o' lanterns became part of the celebration of Halloween, but most of these books and websites provide very little in the way of documentation for these explanations. Regardless, the jack o' lantern would be firmly associated with Halloween by the 19th Century.

According to the *Oxford English Dictionary*, the phrase "jack o' lantern" originated in the 17th Century. It was in 1663 that the phrase "Jack with the lantern" first appeared in print. Its original meaning was that of "a man carrying a lantern; a night watchman." In a few years "Jack with the lantern" would evolve into the more familiar "jack o' lantern". Both "jack with the lantern" and "jack o' lantern" are two of a number of phrases in English in which "jack" was used of any man in general. Similar phrases are "jack of all trades" for someone with a wide number of skills or "Jack the lad" for a boisterous, overconfident, young man.

Also according to the *Oxford English Dictionary*, by 1673 the phrase "jack o' lantern" was being applied to the phenomenon of the ignis fatuus, more commonly called in English "will o' the wisp", as well. The will o' the wisp is a light that sometimes appears over marshy land, created by the combustion of gas from decomposing organic matter.

The phrase "jack o' lantern" would not be applied to carved vegetables into which candles are placed until the 19th Century. One of the earliest possible uses in print (perhaps <u>the</u> earliest use) of "jack o' lantern" for a carved vegetable with a candle inside it appears in Samuel Taylor Coleridge's review of Charles Maturin's play *Bertram* in 1817, "The characters in this act frisk about, here, there, and everywhere, as teasingly as Jack o' Lantern lights which mischievous boys, from across a narrow street, throw with a looking-glass on the faces of their opposite neighbours." Unfortunately, while it seems likely that Coleridge is referring to carved vegetables into which candles are placed, it is not entirely clear. He could easily have been referring to something else.

Fortunately William Holloway's *A General Dictionary of Provincialisms* (published in 1838) would be very clear on the topic. Under the entry for "jack in the lantern" he writes, "In Hampshire, boys, of a dark night, get a large turnip and scooping out the inside, make two holes in it to resemble eyes and one for a mouth, when they place a lighted candle within side, and put it on a wall or a post so that it may appear like the head of a man. The chief end (and that a very bad one) is to take some younger boy than the rest, and who is not in the secret, to show it to him, with a view to frighten him." That carved vegetables were already in use in the United States and referred to as "jack o' lanterns" by the mid-19th Century is made clear by Nathaniel Hawthorne in his novel

House of the Seven Gables (published in 1851). In the book one character suggests to another with regards to the Great Carbuncle, "Hide it under that cloak, say'st thou? Why, it will gleam through the holes, and make thee look like a Jack o'lanthern!"

While it seems clear that the phrase "jack o' lantern" was being used of vegetables carved for use as lanterns by the 19th Century, it is unclear where or when the practice of doing so originated. Despite the many claims made for Ireland, the earliest references to these vegetable lanterns come from England and Scotland. In 1756 *The British, Roman, and Saxon antiquities and folklore of Worcestershire* by antiquarian Jabez Allies makes reference to turnip lanterns called "Hoberdy's Lanterns" he remembered from his youth. He wrote, "In my juvenile days I remember to have seen peasant boys make, what they called a 'Hoberdy's Lantern,' by hollowing out a turnip, and cutting eyes, nose, and mouth therein, in the true moon-like style; and having lighted it up by inserting the stump of a candle, they used to place it upon a hedge to frighten unwary travellers in the night." Such turnip lanterns were also being made in North America. In the November 21 1778 issue of *The Pennsylvania Packet*, there is a reference to a boy's "turnip lanthorn...with a little bit of candle in it."

Of course, so far none of the sources refer to turnip lanterns or jack o' lanterns as being associated with Halloween. What could be the earliest reference to turnip lanterns and Halloween occurs in the *Etymological Dictionary of the Scottish Language* by Scottish antiquarian John Jamieson (published in

1808). In the dictionary there is an entry for "Candle and Castock". The entry reads "a large turnip, from which the top is sliced off that it may be hollowed out till the rind become transparent: a candle is then put into it, the top being restored by way of lid or cover. The light shows in a frightful manner the face formed with blacking on the outside, S. Hence the rhyme of children: 'Halloween, a night at e'en, A candle in a castock'. These, being sometimes placed in church-yards, on Allhallow eve, are supposed to have given rise to many of the tales of terror believed by the vulgar." At least in early 19th Century Scotland, then, what was called a "candle and castock" (what would later be called a "jack o' lantern") had an association with Halloween.

As to how turnip lanterns became associated with Halloween, it would seem there could be a simple explanation for that. The custom of pulling pranks on Halloween dates back to at least the 18th Century in the Scottish Highlands and Ireland. Both Jabez Allies and William Holloway make reference to turnip lanterns being used to frighten people. It would not take much imagination for pranksters on Halloween to decide to scare people with turnip lanterns carved to resemble a human face.

It was in North America that pumpkins would overtake turnips as the preferred vegetables for making jack o' lanterns. Pumpkins are native to North America and were cultivated by various Native American tribes. It would not be long after Europeans began colonising North America that they would also begin raising pumpkins. Pumpkins are harvested in autumn, so it was quite natural that the vegetable would become associated with the season. Not only are pumpkins harvested at autumn, but they are also much easier to carve than turnips.

Of course, while the pumpkin would become the preferred vegetable for carving jack o' lanterns, it would be some time before they would become firmly associated with Halloween. What may be the first image of a pumpkin carved as a jack o' lantern occurred in the November 23 1867 issue of *Harper's Weekly*. The engraving, titled "The Pumpkin Effigy", made no reference to Halloween and that issue of *Harper's Weekly* came out at Thanksgiving, not Halloween.

Regardless, by the 1890s the carving of pumpkins for jack o' lanterns would be a firmly established custom at Halloween in the United States. The practice was regularly referenced in newspaper articles from the decade. By the 1900s the image of pumpkins carved as jack o' lanterns would appear frequently on Halloween postcards. That having been said, as late as the early 20th Century people were still using other vegetables than pumpkins to make jack o' lanterns as well. In her 1912 book *Games for Halloween*, Mary E. Blain makes reference to jack o' lanterns "..made from apples, cucumbers, squash, pumpkins, etc."

Of course, by the 1900s not only were jack o' lanterns appearing on Halloween postcards, but paper manufacturers were making paper decorations in the shape of jack o' lanterns. Many of these were made in Germany, but American companies soon joined in as well. The Dennison Manufacturing Company began making paper Halloween decorations, including jack o' lanterns, in the 1900s. Their Halloween decorations were so popular that in 1909 Dennison published its first *Dennison's Bogie Book for Halloween*, which was a guide for decorating for the holiday. Another *Dennison's Bogie Book* would be published in 1912. With the exception of the years of World War I, it would then be published annually until 1934. Another American company well known for their paper Halloween decorations, including jack o' lanterns, is the Beistle Company. Founded in 1900, the Beistie Company began making Halloween decorations in 1920. Over the years the Beistle Company has made several different Halloween decorations in the shape of jack o' lanterns.

It was in the early Fifties that plastic decorations in the shape of jack o' lanterns were introduced. The earliest of these decorations were simple jack o' lanterns with electric lights inside that would sit on a table or shelf. As time passed a wide variety of plastic jack o' lantern themed merchandise emerged. There were flashlights, lawn ornaments, candy containers, and so on. Blow mould lawn ornaments reached their peak in popularity in the Sixties. The wide array of plastic jack o' lantern goods (many of which are still manufactured) were made by a number of companies, including Union Products, Empire Plastic Corp., Gregg Products, and others.

It was in 2001 that novelty and seasonal products company Gemmy Industries introduced inflatable lawn ornaments under the name "Airblown Inflatables". Among their first offerings in 2001 was an inflatable jack o' lantern. As inflatable seasonal decorations grew in popularity in the Naughts (and became an outright craze in 2006), other companies would make their own inflatable decorations, including jack o' lanterns. Since 2001 Gemmy Industries itself has introduced several variations on the jack o' lantern theme, including stacked jack o' lanterns and jack o' lanterns with licensed characters (such as Jack Skellington from *The Nightmare Before Christmas*).

Given how strongly linked to Halloween jack o' lanterns have become, it would come as no surprise that they would play a role in popular culture. One of the earliest instances of this is the character of Jack Pumpkinhead, who first appeared in L. Frank Baum's book *The Marvellous Land of Oz*. As his name suggests, he has a jack o' lantern for a head. While jack o' lanterns are not referenced in Washington Irving's short story "The Legend of Sleepy Hollow", depictions of the Headless Horseman often depict him as having a jack o' lantern in place of his severed head (a well -known example of this can be seen in Disney's 1949 adaptation of the short story). In the movie *Arsenic and Old Lace* Aunts Abby and Martha give jack o' lanterns to trick-or-treaters as "treats". While Charles Schulz never actually portrayed the imaginary character Linus calls the Great Pumpkin in the comic strip *Peanuts* or in the famous TV special *It's the Great Pumpkin, Charlie Brown*, in parodies it is often portrayed as a jack o' lantern. At any rate, appearances of jack o' lanterns in pop culture occur so frequently that it would be difficult to list every single instance.

It is impossible to say precisely where and when what would later be called jack o' lanterns emerged. It is not even clear exactly how they became identified with Halloween. Regardless, by the late 19th Century the jack o' lantern was firmly associated with the holiday and by the early 20th Century it would become one of Halloween's most popular symbols. Indeed, today it is difficult to think of a time when there was Halloween without jack o' lanterns.

A Brief History of Trick-or-Treating

Perhaps no other custom is as closely identified with Halloween in the United States and Canada as trick-or-treating. The U.S. Census Bureau estimated that 41.2 million children went from door to door asking for treats in 2014. An estimated $3 billion is spent on candy alone each Halloween. Given how strongly identified trick-or-treating is with Halloween in the United States and Canada, one would think it had <u>always</u> been a part of the holiday. That having been said, while Halloween is a fairly old holiday, trick-or-treating itself only goes back as far as the 20th Century.

Of course, this is not to say that there were not customs similar to trick-or-treating that pre-date the 20th Century, although often they were associated with holidays other than Halloween. In England wassailing was a practice that dates back to the Middle Ages. It was observed at Twelfth Night and involved people going from door to door singing and offering a drink of wassail (generally a hot mulled punch) in exchange for gifts. In many ways it was a forerunner to carolling. Mumming is another Yuletide custom that dates back to the Middle Ages. It involves people going from door to door asking for food or money in exchange for a performance of a mummer's play. Allhallowtide (Halloween, All Saints' Day, and All Souls' Day) had its own equivalent custom in the form of souling. Souling was a custom observed in England, Ireland, Scotland, and Wales on

All Souls' Day whereby individuals would go from door to door singing and praying for those who have died in exchange for soul cakes. At least from the 16th Century a similar custom was observed in Scotland on Halloween itself. Guising consisted of groups of young men setting about in costumes and singing in exchange for nuts, apples, or money.

While these customs are quite similar to today's trick-or-treating, a direct line cannot be traced from trick-or-treating back to any of them. The first book-length history of Halloween, *The Book of Hallowe'en* by Ruth Edna Kelley, was published in 1919. Ruth Edna Kelley was very extensive when it came to the many customs, tricks, games, and other forms of revelry with which Halloween was observed in the United States at the time. She makes no mention of trick-or-treating or any ritual even resembling it.

Of course, while trick-or-treating might not have existed (or at least was not widely practised) in the United States in 1919, tricks were a well-established Halloween tradition. Playing pranks while wearing costumes on Halloween dates back to at least the 18th Century in the Scottish Highlands and Ireland. Scottish and Irish immigrants quite naturally brought the tradition of Halloween tricks to the United States. Among the stranger pranks described in Ruth Edna Kelley's *The Book of Hallowe'en* is bags of flour being dumped on passers-by. This odd custom is also referenced by Sally Benson in her semi-autobiographical vignette "October, 1903", one of the vignettes in her series *5135 Kensington*. First published in the November 1 1941 issue of *The New Yorker* and included in the 1942 book *Meet in St.*

Louis, the vignette describes a custom whereby individuals are hit with flour and said to be "killed". This custom would later be portrayed in the musical based on the book, *Meet Me in St. Louis* (1944).

From ringing doorbells and hitting people with flour there would not seem to be too much of a leap from threatening people with pranks (that is, "tricks") if they do not hand over treats. Quite simply, at some point in the early 20th Century perhaps some enterprising child or group of children realised that they could use the threat of the typical pranks performed at Halloween as a means of getting treats in return. Don't want your windows soaped or your outhouse turned over? Then hand over the goodies! Indeed, this would explain the origin of the phrase "trick or treat" quite easily. Of course, here it must be pointed out that we really don't know how or why trick-or-treating came about at all.

While trick-or-treating is often thought of as an American custom, the first known use of the phrase "trick-or-treat" in print came from Blackie, Alberta in Canada. In the November 4 1927 issue of the *Herald* (published in Lethbridge, Alberta) there appeared an article entitled, "'Trick or Treat' Is Demand." After mentioning the usual, harmless pranks pulled at Halloween, the article states, "The youthful tormentors were at back door and front demanding edible plunder by the word 'trick or treat' to which the inmates gladly responded and sent the robbers away rejoicing."

Curiously, while the phrase "trick-or-treat" is first mentioned in Canada in 1927, it is not until 1934 that it is first mentioned in the United States. In fact, 1934 seems to be a bit of a banner year for the custom, with no less than two newspapers referencing trick-or-treating and another describing what would seem to be trick-or-treating, even though the phrase "trick-or-treating" is not used. The first article, "Halloween Pranks Keep Police on Hop", was from the November 1 1934 *Oregon Journal* (published in Portland). There it was reported, "Other young goblins and ghosts, employing modern shakedown methods, successfully worked the 'trick or treat' system in all parts of the city." The second article, "The Gangsters of Tomorrow", from the November 2 1934 issue of the *The Helena Independent* in Montana, described how a child would "...give a citizen every opportunity to comply with his demands before pulling any rough stuff." The article gives an unusual variation of the now traditional exhortation, "Madam, we are here for the usual purpose, 'trick or treat.'"

While both the *Oregon Journal* and *The Helena Independent* characterise trick-or-treating in terms suggesting a form of extortion, the November 3 1934 "Front Views and Profiles" column by June Provines in *The Chicago Tribune* treats the young custom slightly more positively. Although neither the terms "trick-or-treat" nor "trick-or-treating" appear, it would seem the author is clearly describing the custom. Quite simply, Miss Provines writes that the children of Aurora, Illinois "..have a unique way of celebrating Halloween. Instead of soaping windows and ringing doorbells they get into costume and go from door to door asking for handouts." She notes that if "...no contribution is forthcoming they soap the windows in revenge." Although the words "trick-or-treat" never appear, the "Front Views and Profiles" column is clearly describing trick-or-treating.

Much like the earliest articles in the *Herald* from Lethbridge, Alberta, the *Oregon Journal*, and *The Helena Independent*, various accounts of trick-or-treating in American newspapers in the Thirties tended to describe the custom in terms that bring to mind extortion or other rackets associated with gangsters. The title of an article from the November 1 1938 issue of *The Reno Evening Gazette* in Nevada was simply, "Youngsters Shakedown Residents". An article from the October 30 1938 issue of *The Los Angeles Times*, "Halloween Pranks Plotted by Youngsters of Southland", refers to groups of trick-or-treaters as "diminutive Halloween goon squads". While many articles couched trick-or-treating in such terms, there were also many articles on the custom from the Thirties that seem sympathetic to the trick-or-treaters. Much of the reason that trick-or-treating was treated sympathetically by many adults at the time could be that with the adoption of trick-or-treating there appears to have been a reduction in the usual sorts of vandalism that had characterised Halloween in the late 19th and early 20th Centuries. For example, the aforementioned article from *The Reno Evening Gazette* noted that it was "... one of the quietest Halloweens on record."

As to the treats children "extorted" from adults in the Thirties at Halloween, they were not always the candy that is usually handed out today. The aforementioned *Oregon Journal* article notes, "Many women have some apples, cookies or doughnuts for them." The aforementioned "Front Views and

Profiles" column from *The Chicago Tribune* reported that the children are "..given pop corn balls, apples, or candy." The aforementioned *Los Angeles Times* article notes trick-or-treaters "...are bought off with cookies, candy, tickless alarm clocks or the price of an ice cream cone." It would appear in the Thirties that treats often varied and many times (such as the popcorn balls) they were home-made.

Of course, from the very beginning trick-or-treating has involved children dressing up in costumes. In the early days of trick-or-treating Halloween costumes would often be home-made. As might be expected, such traditional Halloween favourites as ghosts, witches, devils, and skeletons were popular in the Thirties. Also popular were clowns (although not of the creepy kind), cowboys, police officers, and assorted other occupations as choices for costumes. That having been said, even as trick-or-treating took hold in the United States and Canada in the Thirties, children's choices in costumes were beginning to change. Such companies as Ben Cooper, Collegevile, and Halco had entered the Halloween costume industry in the Twenties and Thirties. By the Thirties they had started manufacturing costumes of licensed characters. From 1935 to 1938 Halco made costumes based on the characters from the comic strip *Thimble Theatre*, including Popeye, Olive Oyl, and Wimpy. Starting in 1937, Ben Cooper produced costumes of various Walt Disney characters under F. S. Fishbach, Inc.'s "Spotlight" label. During the Thirties Collegeville manufactured a "Lone Ranger" costume.

Today it is not unusual for trick-or-treaters to be accompanied by adults, but in the Thirties this does not seem to be the case. Indeed, from the earliest articles it would appear that trick-or-treating was instigated by the youngsters themselves (*The Chicago Tribune's* "Front Views and Profiles" column from November 3 1934 being an example). The earliest articles about trick-or-treating do not mention adults accompanying trick-or-treaters on their rounds What is more, it appears from the earliest articles children had to actually explain the whole concept of "trick-or-treating" to adults.

It would also appear that from the first references to trick-or-treating in the United States that it was originally a phenomenon in the West and the Mid-West. The three earliest references to trick-or-treating in the United States are from Oregon, Montana, and Illinois. As the Thirties progressed, reports of trick-or-treating began to appear further and further east. There was a story in *The Hammond Times* in Indiana on October 31 1938. There was a story on trick-or-treating in *The Oil City Derrick* in Pennsylvania on October 29 1939. By the late Thirties or early Forties trick-or-treating appears to have reached the East Coast. There was an article on trick-or-treating in *The Cumberland Evening Times* in Maryland on October 24 1942.

It was in 1939 that the first reference to trick-or-treating occurred in a national publication. It was in the article "A Victim of the Window Soaping Brigade?" by Doris Hudson Moss in the November 1939 issue of *The American Home*. The article detailed her success over the past few years in hosting trick-or-treaters. Another early reference from a national publication occurred in a 1941 issue of the magazine *Gleanings in Bee Culture*, wherein it included "some toothsome recipes for some honey goodies that you can hand out to these would-be pranksters."

Not only would national publications take greater notice of trick-or-treating as the Forties progressed, but it was not long before the candy industry took notice as well. In the 1942 annual report for Brach's it was noted, "As one of the three biggest candy occasions of the year, Halloween found Brach's ready with a full line for the Trick or Treat set." By the mid to late Forties candy manufacturers were taking full advantage of trick-or-treating to sell their products. The advertising of Curtiss Candy Company, Mars, and other candy companies in the mid to late Forties often referenced trick-or-treating. It would not be long before candy would be the chosen treat given out to trick-or-treaters.

Candy manufacturers weren't the only advertisers to capitalise on trick-or-treating. A 1946 advertisement for the soft drink featured a couple greeting trick-or-treaters at their door with bottles of 7 Up. A 1950 ad for Coca-Cola featured a jack o' lantern filled with bottles of Coca-Cola and the slogan "Treat 'em right with Coke!"

It should perhaps not be surprising that the earliest references to trick-or-treating in pop culture stem from the Forties. What might possibly be the first reference to trick-or-treating in film occurred in the classic comedy *Arsenic and Old Lace* (1944). Although the film was shot in 1941, Warner Bros. delayed the release of *Arsenic and Old Lace* until the stage play (upon which it was based) finished its run. Early in the film there is a scene in which Aunts Abby and Martha give trick-or-treaters at their door two carved pumpkins. Following the war trick-or-treating would also be referenced on popular radio shows. Trick or treating was at the centre of the plot of November 1 1946 episode, "Halloween Show", of *The Baby Snooks Show*. Trick-or-treating also played a role in the plots of the episode "Jack Goes Trick or Treating" of *The Jack Benny Programme* (which aired on October 31 1948) and the episode "Haunted House" of *The Adventures of Ozzie and Harriet* (which also aired on October 31 1948).

By the late Forties and early Fifties trick-or-treating had become an established custom that was observed nationwide in the United States. It was in 1950 that the fundraising programme Trick-or-Treat for UNICEF began. It was in 1949 that Mary Emma Allison, a pastor's wife, observed a UNICEF booth taking a collection for funds to send powdered milk to malnourished children around the world. It occurred to Mrs. Allison that children could collect for UNICEF while trick-or-treating. She then enlisted both her own children and the children in her community to collect money for UNICEF on Halloween in 1950. It was in 1953 that the United States Committee for UNICEF began actively promoting the campaign. The campaign had spread throughout the nation by the Sixties, and in 1967 President Lyndon B. Johnson declared October 31 to be "UNICEF Day" in the United States. Trick-or-Treat for UNICEF would play a central role in the plot of the *Bewitched* episode "To Trick-Or-Treat or Not to Trick-Or-Treat" that aired on October 30 1969.

Given the prevalence of trick-or-treating in the Fifties, it should come as no surprise that it was referenced in the popular culture of the era. The October 31 1952 episode of *The Adventures of Ozzie and Harriet*, "Halloween Party", portrayed the Nelsons as besieged by trick-or-treaters. It was that same year that Walt Disney released the classic Donald Duck animated short "Trick or Treat". As might be expected, the candy industry continued to exploit the holiday. A 1953 ad for Dubble Bubble Gum featured a cartoon of a woman handing out treats to youngsters with the slogan, "Treat the kids on Halloween with Fleer's Dubble Bubble Gum." A 1955 Mars ad stated, "When 'TRICKS OR TREATS' is the question, here are two perfect answers: Mars 6-Packs--Mars '24s'."

From the Fifties into the Sixties there would be a shift in the sort of costumes children wore while trick-or-treating. Following the end of World War II costumes of licensed characters manufactured by Ben Cooper, Collegeville, and Halco became a popular choice for many youngsters. The shift from children's tastes in costumes from the traditional ghosts and goblins to the latest television heroes was significant enough to be noted in an Associated Press article by Sid Moody published on October 31 1960. In the article, Harry Mirsky, a representative for J. Halpern Company (better known as Halco), is quoted as saying, "Oh, we still sell devil suits, and witches and hobgoblins, but we're getting away from those weirdies. Television did it. Nowadays kids don't want to be skeletons. They want to dress up like the characters they see on TV." Ben Cooper and Collegeville would continue to dominate the Halloween costume market into the Nineties.

As prevalent as trick-or-treating had become in the Fifties, it was perhaps inevitable that urban legends surrounding the custom would arise. Namely, the early Sixties saw the emergence of rumours of poisoned candy being handed out at Halloween. It is difficult to say why these rumours came about, although they may have originated in 1959 with a California dentist named William Shyne. That year William Shyne handed out 450 laxative tablets to trick-or-treaters. About thirty of them ate the tablets and became sick. Dr. Shyne was charged with "outrage of public decency" and "unlawful dispensing of drugs" It seems possible that the tale of William Shyne distributing laxative tablets to trick-or-treaters could have gotten misconstrued as poison candy being distributed. Regardless, urban legends of poisoned candy persisted from the Sixties well into the Eighties. Despite this, according to sociologist Joel Best of the University of Delaware (who did an in-depth study of the phenomenon), there appears to be nearly no evidence of strangers randomly handing out poisoned candy to children on Halloween.

Of course, the urban legends regarding poisoned candy were probably helped greatly by a murder case in Houston, Texas in 1974. On October 31 1974 eight-year-old Timothy Marc O'Bryan died from eating Pixie Stix laced with cyanide. As it turned out, the young boy was given the Pixie Stix by his own father, Ronald Clark O'Bryan, who also gave cyanide-laced Pixie Stix to his daughter and three other children. Fortunately none of the other youngsters ate the Pixie Stix. The police soon figured out that Ronald Clark O'Bryan was the culprit as none of the houses visited were handing out Pixie Stix. Sadly, it seems that Timothy Marc O'Bryan's own father had murdered him for insurance money. Ronald Clark O'Bryan was executed by lethal injection on March 31 1984.

It was around 1967 that urban legends of sharp objects in trick-or-treat candy (needles, pins, razor blades, etc.) began to overtake the urban legends of poisoned candy. While these urban legends about sharp objects in Halloween candy would be prevalent throughout the late Sixties and into the Eighties, according to Joel Best every single instance of such candy tampering since 1959 has proven to be a hoax. Not only does it seem that there are not people randomly handing out poisoned candy to children at Halloween, there aren't people randomly handing out candy filled with needles or pins or razor blades either.

Unfortunately in 1982 trick or treating would feel the impact of a real life case of product tampering, although it had nothing to do with Halloween. On September 29 1982 a twelve year old Illinois girl died after taking a capsule of Extra-Strength Tylenol that had been laced with cyanide. Over the next few days six more people in the Chicago area died from cyanide laced doses of Tylenol. On October 5 1982 Johnson & Johnson issued a nationwide recall of Tylenol products.

As the first major case of product tampering in American history, the Chicago Tylenol murders would result in pharmaceutical companies developing new, tamper resistant packaging. It would also have a serious impact on the holiday of Halloween as it was celebrated in 1982. Many parents, worried that similar product tampering might happen with regards to candy, refused to take their children out trick-or-treating that year. Cities in New Jersey, Ohio, Pennsylvania, Illinois, and Massachusetts outright banned trick-or-treating. Stores across the nation reported that candy sales had dropped 20 to 50 percent. The Tylenol scare even affected Halloween costume manufacturers, such as Ben Cooper and Collegeville, who saw their sales drop precipitously.

Fortunately Halloween and trick-or-treating would rebound from the Tylenol Scare. In 1983 eight different Halloween costume manufacturers and the Toy Manufacturers of America formed the Halloween Celebration Committee in an effort to save the holiday. The Halloween Celebration Committee published a pamphlet entitled "13 Great Ways to Celebrate Halloween" in an effort to revitalise the holiday. Candy sales rebounded in 1984 and trick-or-treating resumed as it had in previous years.

That is not to say that trick-or-treating would not continue to change and evolve. The Eighties would see a trend towards latex masks of the sort Don Post Studios had made since 1938 and a concurrent trend towards more realistic, more sophisticated costumes. Ben Cooper went out of business in the early Nineties. Collegeville was bought by younger rival company Rubies Costume Company at auction in 1996. The Nineties saw a return to people making their own costumes, and those costumes manufactured by costume companies were generally more realistic than the plastic masks and plastic smocks of the sort made by Ben Cooper, Collegeville, and Halco in the mid-20th Century.

There also developed a variant on trick-or-treating known as trunk-or-treat. Trunk-or-treating is a community event wherein children go from car to car in a parking lot, usually that of a school, church, city hall, or other community building. It is not known precisely where the first trunk-or-treat event was held, much less who came up with the idea or how they came up with it. It does seems as if it was a particularly attractive alternative for those churches that regarded Halloween as a "pagan" festival and trick-or-treating with it (at such churches children are encouraged to dress as characters from the Bible). Regardless, trunk-or-treating appears to have developed sometime in the mid-Nineties and exploded in popularity in 2006. Since then many communities in the United States and Canada have held their own "trunk-or-treat" events, even though trick-or-treating often continues to take place in those communities as well.

It has been 89 years since the phrase "trick-or-treat" first appeared in print. While trick-or-treating has changed over the years, there is little sign that it is declining in popularity. The American Retail Federation estimated that Americans would spend $2.1 to $2.6 billion on Halloween candy and $2.5 billion on costumes in 2015. Trick-or-treating is nearing its 100th anniversary, but it shows no sign of going out of style.

Ben Cooper & Its Competitors: The Folks Who Sold Halloween

If you were a child anywhere from 1945 to 1990 in the United States, even if you never wore one of their costumes, the chances are very good that you are familiar with Ben Cooper Inc., for a time the biggest maker of Halloween costumes in America. Chances are also very good that you might be familiar with their competitors, Collegeville and Halco. From the mid to late 20th Century Ben Cooper Inc. and its two chief rivals manufactured the bulk of Halloween costumes for children. The costumes were sold at many different stores, including Woolworths's, Montgomery Ward, Sear's, J. C. Penney, and most dime stores. For many in the Silent Generation, the Baby Boom, and Generation X, then, Ben Cooper Inc. is nearly synonymous with the holiday.

Ben Cooper Inc. was founded by Benjamin Cooper. He was the son of a restaurant owner born in 1906 on New York City's Lower East Side. He was only seven years old when he received his first Halloween costume, that of a little devil. While he studied accounting, Ben Cooper's real interests were of a more artistic bent. For a brief time he was a songwriter on Tin Pan Alley. In 1927 he moved from song writing to the theatrical costume business. He designed costumes for the showgirls at the Cotton Club and later costumes for the Ziegfeld Follies.

Broadway and vaudeville shows would go into decline with the Great Depression. It is perhaps for that reason that Ben Cooper founded Ben Cooper Inc. in Brooklyn, New York in 1937. That same year Ben Cooper Inc. took control of F. S. Fishbach, Inc., a wise move given the company had the licence to produce costumes based on Walt Disney characters from Mickey Mouse to Snow White. Starting in 1937, then, Ben Cooper produced costumes of various Walt Disney characters under F. S. Fishbach, Inc.'s "Spotlight" label. While Ben Cooper Inc. and F. S. Fishbach, Inc. were more or less one company starting in 1937, they would not formally merge until 1942, when they were incorporated as "Ben Cooper Inc."

As surprising as it might seem to Baby Boomers and Gen Xers given Ben Cooper's dominance of the Halloween costume industry from the Fifties to the Sixties, it was not the oldest company to make Halloween costumes, nor was it the first Halloween costume manufacturer to engage in licensing. As early as 1916 crepe paper manufacturer Dennison offered disposable, paper, Halloween costumes. In fact, Ben Cooper Inc.'s chief rival for many decades, Collegeville Flag and Manufacturing Company, pre-dated it by many years. Collegeville Flag was founded in Collegeville, Pennsylvania in 1910 as a manufacturer of flags and aprons. They entered the costume business very early. One source states that it was 1920, while others simply say that it entered the costume business in the early Twenties. Regardless, the story goes that Collegeville Flag found they had excess material on hand and as a result they manufactured their first costume--a clown costume.

Not only would Collegeville enter the costume business at a very early date, they were also one of the first costume companies to deal with licensed characters. As early as the late Thirties they made a Lone Ranger costume.

Not only was Collegeville an older company than Ben Cooper, Inc., but so was its other chief rival, Halco. Halco was founded in 1917 as the J. Halpern Company, a company that dealt in toys, novelties, stationery, and so on. For much of the Twentieth Century Halco would be the most respected name in the manufacture of toy cap guns. From cap guns and holsters it would only be a small step for Halco to move into the costume business. Like Collegeville, Halco would also be one of the first costume companies to delve into licensing. From 1935 to 1938 the company made costumes based on the characters from *Thimble Theatre*, including Popeye, Olive Oyl, and Wimpy. They would also start making goods for another holiday, Christmas. Halco manufactured Santa Claus suits, as well as aluminium icicles for Christmas trees.

While all three companies were founded prior to World War II, it would be following the war that the manufacture of Halloween costumes would become a big business. It would also be in the Fifties that children's tastes in costumes would change. Prior to and during World War II, the most popular costumes tended to be those most traditionally associated with Halloween: ghosts, witches, monsters, devils, and so on. While television in the United States had existed since the Thirties, both the Great Depression and World War II prevented regular television broadcasts, let alone any expansion of the medium. It was then in the late Forties that regularly scheduled, network broadcasting began. By the Fifties television had overtaken radio as Americans' medium of choice. As a result Ben Cooper Inc., Collegeville Flag, and Halco based more and more costumes on licensed properties from television shows as the Fifties progressed. The shift from children's tastes in costumes from the traditional ghosts and goblins to the latest television heroes was significant enough to be noted in an Associated Press article by Sid Moody published on 31 October 1960. In the article, Harry Mirsky, a representative for J. Halpern Company, is quoted as saying, "Oh, we still sell devil suits, and witches and hobgoblins, but we're getting away from those weirdies. Television did it. Nowadays kids don't want to be skeletons. They want to dress up like the characters they see on TV."

Given the demand for costumes based on television characters, Ben Cooper, Inc., Collegeville, and Halco would go into licensed characters in a big way in the Fifties. As would be typical for the three companies' histories, Ben Cooper cornered a lion's share of the licensing market in the Fifties. In addition to the Disney character costumes they had been making since the late Thirties, they also manufactured costumes based on such comic book and television characters as Superman, Bat Masterson, Davy Crockett, Paladin (from *Have Gun--Will Travel*), Zorro, and even Rin Tin Tin. Collegeville made costumes based on Warner Brothers cartoon characters, Famous Studios/Harvey Comics characters (Casper the Friendly Ghost and so on), Popeye and related characters, Mandrake the

Magician, characters from *Space Patrol*, and Bret Maverick (from *Maverick*). Halco had its share of licensed characters too, such as various characters from Terrytoons (such as Mighty Mouse), Steve Canyon, the characters from *Gunsmoke*, and The Chipmunks.

Of course, here it should be pointed out that while Ben Coooper Inc. was best known for Halloween costumes, it would expand into making a few toys as well. The company made a variety of playsuits that were often more realistic and sophisticated than its Halloween costumes. In the Fifties they made playsuits for Superman, Bat Masterson, and Zorro. In the Sixties, with Batmania sweeping the United States, they manufactured a Batman playsuit. One of their more enduring toys was Jigglers. Jigglers were rubber figures with strings attached that would jiggle when one bounced the strings up and down. Initially the Jigglers were of traditional Halloween figures (bats, skeletons, and so on), although they would expand to include superheroes and other characters. They also manufactured a series of rubber toys called "Creature People (essentially a cross between a human and some creepy critter)" and even toy cars (their "Lock-Ups" series).

While licensing would come to dominate the Halloween costume industry during the Fifties, it would become an absolute gold rush during the Sixties. While Ben Cooper Inc. would continue to look to television for licensed properties during the Sixties, the company also looked to comic books. Superman had been a popular costume throughout the Fifties, and in 1964 he would be joined by Batman.

Ben Cooper Inc. would even be responsible for the first bit of merchandise under the Marvel Comics imprint. Throughout the Fifties Ben Cooper had made its own "Spiderman" costume. When Marvel Comics introduced Spider-Man in *Amazing Fantasy* #15, August 1962, they naturally trademarked the name. This meant Ben Cooper could no longer use the name "Spiderman" for a costume. Given that was the case, Ben Cooper simply licensed Spider-Man from Marvel Comics and created the first Spider-Man Halloween costume. The character had only had his own title for a few months at that time! By 1966 Ben Cooper's line of superhero costumes would include not only Superman, Batman, and Spider-Man, but also characters such as Green Lantern, The Flash, Captain America, and Thor. Ben Cooper Inc. would even become the first company to trademark the word "super hero," so important was their superhero line in their sales in the mid-Sixties.

Of course, Ben Cooper Inc. made more than superhero costumes in the Sixties. They continued to manufacture costumes based on television properties, including *The Beverly Hillbillies*, *The Flintstones*, *Bewitched*, *Astro Boy*, *Dark Shadows*, *Daniel Boone*, and many more. In 1963 the company even introduced its first costumes based on real people, namely President John F. Kennedy and First Lady Jackie Kennedy. Following JFK's assassination on November 22 1963, the company had to destroy literally thousands of the costumes. In 1964 they would introduce their now much sought after costumes of The Beatles. It was also in the Sixties that Ben Cooper Inc. introduced its Glitter Glo line of costumes (costumes with reflective material that made them easier to see in automobile headlights).

Like Ben Cooper Inc., Collegeville would continue to look to television for costumes. During the Sixties Collegeville made costumes based on such shows as *The Outer Limits, Star Trek* (the much sought after Mr. Spock costume from 1967), *Flipper, Lassie, T.H.E. Cat,* and various others. In addition to the various Warner Brothers characters, Collegeville also made costumes based on such properties as various King Features Syndicate characters (Flash Gordon, The Phantom, Mandrake the Magician), various Harvey Comics characters, (Casper the Friendly Ghost, Wendy the Good Little Witch), The Beatles movie *Yellow Submarine,* and *Mad* magazine mascot Alfred E. Neuman. Halco would also continue to draw inspiration from television, with costumes from such shows as *The Man From U.N.C.L.E., Dr. Kildare, Cimarron Strip, I Love Lucy,* and others. Halco also produced costumes based on a number of other licensed properties, including the comic strip *Dick Tracy,* the action figure G. I. Joe, the action figure Major Matt Mason, the Elizabeth Taylor movie *Cleopatra,* and Tom & Jerry.

Of course, from the Fifties to the Eighties there would still be a place for the traditional ghouls and goblins of Halloween. Throughout the years Ben Cooper Inc., Collegeville, and Halco would produce more than their fair share of witches, ghosts, Frankenstein's Creatures, vampires, zombies, and so on. The licence for the classic Universal Monsters would change from company to company over the years, so that both Ben Cooper Inc. and Collegeville had a chance to make costumes based on Universal's versions of Frankenstein's Creature, Dracula, the Wolf Man, the Creature from the Black Lagoon, and so on. Of course, even when one of the three major companies did not have the rights to the Universal characters, they would produce costumes that were slightly similar. For example, in the mid-Sixties Collegeville produced a costume they simply called "The Monster" that looked similar to Universal's conception of Frankenstein's Creature. Ben Cooper Inc. would do the same when Collegeville had the rights to the Universal Monsters.

The Seventies would see very little change for the three major Halloween costume manufacturers. Ben Cooper Inc. continued to dominate the market and continued to control some of the most desirable licensed properties: DC Comics, Marvel Comics, and the much desired Universal Monsters. Collegeville continued with their usual properties (the Warner Brothers cartoon characters and Harvey Comics characters), as well as putting out costumes based on various Sid and Marty Krofft shows (*H.R. Pufnstuf*). Halco put out costumes based on older television shows (*The Beverly Hillbilllies*), The Lone Ranger, Tom & Jerry, and comic strips such as *Li'l Abner*. Not surprisingly television properties continued to provide the bases for costumes. Ben Cooper manufactured costumes based on such properties as *The Six Million Dollar Man*, *Happy Days*, *Little House on the Prairie*, and *Land of the Lost*. Collegeville put out costumes based on the Gerry Anderson shows *U.F.O.* and *Space: 1999,* as well as *Battlestar Galactica*. Among the stranger costumes of the Seventies were the ones Collegeville based on the band KISS.

One significant development during the Seventies was that the Halloween costumes manufacturers turned increasingly to movies for sources of inspiration. To a degree this was nothing new. Ben Cooper Inc. had been making costumes based on various Disney movie characters since the Thirties (indeed, Snow White was among the earliest movie characters to have a costume based on her). And, of course, theatrical cartoon characters, from Bugs Bunny to Mighty Mouse, had provided fodder for costumes for Collegeville, Halco, and Ben Cooper through the years. In the Sixties, with a spy craze having swept the U.S., Ben Cooper put out a James Bond costume. That having been said, the Seventies saw even more costumes based on movies than any decade before. Collegeville introduced costumes based on such films as *The Golden Voyage of Sinbad*, *Jaws* (as hard as it is to believe), and Ralph Bakshi's animated version of *The Lord of the Rings*. Ben Cooper Inc. would win the *Star Wars* licence, although it only manufactured three costumes based on the film in 1977. They would also make costumes based on *The Planet of the Apes* franchise. Ben Cooper would invite some controversy when they made a costume based on the movie *Alien*, making it the first costume ever based on an R rated movie.

Sadly, the Eighties would not be kind to Ben Cooper Inc. and Collegeville. On September 29 1982 a twelve year old Illinois girl died after taking a capsule of Extra-Strength Tylenol that had been laced with cyanide. Over the course of the next few days six more people in the Chicago area would die from doses of Tylenol that contained cyanide. On October 5 1982 Johnson & Johnson issued a nationwide recall of Tylenol products. As the first major case of product tampering in American history, not only would the Chicago Tylenol murders result in pharmaceutical companies developing new, tamper resistant packaging, but it would have a serious impact on the holiday of Halloween as it was celebrated in 1982. Parents, fearful that similar product tampering might occur with regards to candy, refused to take their children out trick or treating that year. As a result Halloween costume sales dropped dramatically. In 1983 eight different Halloween costume manufacturers (including Ben Cooper) and the Toy Manufacturers of America formed the Halloween Celebration Committee in an effort to save the holiday. The Halloween Celebration Committee published a pamphlet entitled "13 Great Ways to Celebrate Halloween" in an effort to revitalise the holiday.

In the end the Tylenol cyanide scare would prove to only be a bump in the road for Ben Cooper and Collegeville. The sale of Halloween costumes would steadily increase in the years following 1982. Unfortunately, this did not mean that what were once the two top Halloween costume manufacturers would continue to thrive. In particular, Ben Cooper Inc. found itself beginning to fail in the Eighties. The Eighties would see a trend towards latex masks of the sort Don Post Studios had made since 1938 and a concurrent trend towards more realistic, more sophisticated costumes. Once faced only with competition from Collegeveille Flag and J. Halpern Company, in the Eighties Ben Cooper Inc. found itself competing with younger companies such as Rubies Costume Company. Rubies Costume

Company had been founded in 1950 as Rubies Candy Store in Queens, New York. Rubies expanded into novelty and joke products as the Fifties progressed, so that it changed its name to Rubies Fun House in 1959. In 1967 Rubies opened a costume rental department and in 1972 the company changed their name again to Rubies Costume Company. It was in 1973 that they entered into the mass production of Halloween costumes.

In the end the financial difficulties Ben Cooper Inc. experienced in the late Eighties became so severe that the company filed for bankruptcy on March 13 1988. Worse yet, on January 6 1989 a fire broke out at the Ben Cooper's plant in Roseville, Georgia, destroying $ 2 million to $3 million worth of inventory, according to the company. To make matters worse, the Insurance Company of the State of Pennsylvania (with whom Ben Cooper had their coverage) refused to cover the damage, alleging that Ben Cooper Inc. had misrepresented the amount of damage the fire actually caused. Initially the bankruptcy court refused to hear Ben Cooper's claims against ICSP, although the company appealed the court's ruling. Eventually the courts would rule that Ben Cooper's claim against ICSP could be heard by the bankruptcy court.

Ben Cooper Inc. would emerge from bankruptcy in April 1989. Unfortunately, this would not be the end of their problems. In early January 1991 the company was moving from Brooklyn, New York (where they had spent the entirety of their history) to Greensboro, North Carolina so that they could be closer to Southern textile factories. The company planned to put $6 million into their new Greensboro facility and intended to apply for a $600,000 Community Development Block Grant to help with costs. Unfortunately the company would not last. On October 30 1991 (ironically, the day before Halloween), Ben Cooper Inc. once more filed bankruptcy. It was in 1992 that Ben Cooper Inc. was bought out by competitor Rubies Costumes Company. After fifty five years, Ben Cooper Inc. was out of business.

Despite such profitable licences as *The Teenage Mutant Ninja Turtles*; *ET, the Extra-Terrestrial*; *Barney*; and the Universal Monsters, Collegeville would find its fortunes in decline with the Nineties. In 1994 Collegeville took out a good number of loans from Meridian Bank, with the intent of paying them with the profits made from Halloween that year. Unfortunately, that summer Collegeville failed to win the licence for the popular "Power Rangers" franchise. As a result Collegeville's profits fell short by around $10 to $12 million and they defaulted on their loans to Meridian Bank.

It would seem 1994 proved to be a very bad year for Collegeville. That same year a court determined that costumes made by Collegeville and competitor Rubies Costume Company were not flame retardant as claimed and did not comply with the Flammable Fabrics Act (here it must be noted that Ben Cooper Inc. had claimed their costumes were flame retardant for years). In the end both companies had to pay $75,000 in court costs and civil penalties from the lawsuits. In the end Rubies Costume Company bought Collegeville at an auction in 1996.

As to J. Halpern Company, in 1967 it was merged into Kusan Inc., a manufacturer of die cast and plastic products for cars, appliances, toys, and so on. Kusan Inc. closed the J. Halpern division in 1977, after which it was bought by its current ownership. Halco survives to this day, primarily manufacturing Santa Claus suits, as well as costumes for Santa's helpers and the Easter Bunny.

While many Baby Boomers and Gen Xers have fond memories of the costumes manufactured by Ben Cooper Inc., Collegeville, and Halco, they also admit the downsides of those costumes. The plastic smocks (I've also heard them called "jumpsuits") were, at most, made in only three sizes: small, medium, and large. For that reason it was very rare that a costume fit the child wearing it, and many children found they had to wear them over their clothes. They also were not very comfortable.

It was also a rare thing that a costume actually resembled the garb worn by any particular character. Characters such as Superman, Batman, and The Green Hornet, whose costumes somewhat resembled the suits they wore in the comic books or on television, were the exception to the rule. Usually the costumes (particularly those made by Ben Cooper) would portray a scene with the character on the smock. Even when a costume resembled that worn by a character, the name would be printed boldly on the costume (in the case of Batman, it was in the centre of the bat insignia). The masks that came with the costume were made of moulded plastic and held on by a thin, white, elastic band. By and large they were uncomfortable to wear. Even on a cold day they were hot, so that sweat would eventually build up on one's face. It was also often hard to breathe while wearing the mask.

Whatever the shortcomings of the costumes made by Ben Cooper, Collegeville, and Halco, they also had several advantages. First and foremost, they were affordable. In 1963 a Halco costume could be bought for as little as $1.49 (about $10.80 in 2011). Second, they were convenient. Today we tend to think of the late Forties to the Seventies as a more relaxed time when people were not so busy. And while this might be true to some degree, the fact is that even in the Fifties, Sixties, and Seventies parents often found many demands on their time. For parents with no time to make costumes for their children, then, the mass produced costumes from Ben Cooper, Halco, and Collegevile were an ideal solution. For a few dollars one's child had a costume that required no work on the part of the parent other than buying it at the store.

Third, the costumes from Ben Cooper, Collegeville, and Halco allowed children to be their favourite comic book, comic strip, or television characters with little difficulty. Even for a mother or father who was skilled at sewing, creating a Superman costume could be a daunting task, but for a few dollars one could buy his or her child a Superman costume that somewhat resembled the one worn by the character in comic books. Here I must point out that one could buy masks separately from the costumes, so that one could make his or her own costume and still have a mask that resembled one's favourite character. For instance, a Casper the Friendly Ghost mask from Collegeville could be combined with a white, one piece, footed outfit to create a fairly good Casper the Friendly Ghost costume. Fourth, among Ben Cooper, Colllegeville, and Halco there were a wide variety of costumes to be had. In the Sixties a child could be anything from Mr. Spock to Sgt. Troy from the TV show *Rat Patrol*.

Of course, given that the costumes from Ben Cooper Inc., Collegeville, and Halco were largely similar in terms of how they were made, it seems notable that Ben Cooper Inc. was the leader in the Halloween costume industry for the entirety of its history. Even in 1991, when the company had just emerged from bankruptcy, it still controlled around 70 to 80 percent of the market with regards to Halloween costumes based on licensed characters. Of course, as pointed out above, Ben Cooper Inc. was not the first Halloween costume company to deal with licensed characters--Halco had done so even before Ben Cooper Inc. was founded. I rather suspect that much of the company's success was rooted in the fact that it received the licence to produce costumes based on the Disney characters the very year it was founded. Today, when we largely take the Disney characters for granted, it is easy to forget how popular the various Disney characters were in the Thirties. What is more, the popularity of Disney at the time went well beyond Mickey Mouse and Donald Duck. Until *Gone with the Wind* overtook it, *Snow White & the Seven Dwarfs* was the highest grossing film of all time (when adjusted for inflation it is still in the top ten highest grossing films of all time). Although I have no data to really support this, I have to wonder that the profits that Ben Cooper Inc. made from Disney related costumes did not give them the money to get the rights to the most popular characters when it came to licensing.

Regardless of whether having the licences for Disney proved important in Ben Cooper's success, there was another, perhaps more important factor in the company's dominance of the Halloween costume market. Quite simply, Ben Cooper Inc. had a knack for getting licences for what would become the next big thing. As discussed above, Ben Cooper Inc. bought the rights to create a Spider-Man costume when the character had only had his own title for a few months. While Spider-Man was not well known in 1963, however, he would become one of the most popular comic book characters in only a few years. It was in 1964 that Ben Cooper licensed Batman, a 25 year old character. Two years later the *Batman* TV series would become an outright phenomenon, with merchandise related to the character flying off store shelves. In the Seventies Ben Cooper Inc. received the licences for *Star Wars* characters before *Star Wars* became one of the biggest box office hits of all time. Whether Ben Cooper Inc. simply had an eye for what could become the next big thing or whether there was a good deal of luck involved, the fact that Ben Cooper licensed TV shows and movies before they became popular probably played a role in their dominance of the Halloween costume market.

Having been bought by Rubies Costume Company, Ben Cooper Inc. no longer exists. Also having been bought by Rubies Costume Company, Collegeville exists merely as a division of that company, Collegeville/Imagineering. Halco still exists, but no longer manufactures Halloween costumes.

Regardless, for many the three companies remain synonymous with Halloween. For literally decades they dominated the Halloween costume market to the point that the majority of Halloween costumes may have been made by them. Although two of the companies no longer exist and one no longer makes Halloween costumes, they won't soon be forgotten.

Haunted Houses

The haunted house is one of the most widespread tropes in horror literature, films, and television. It has been the theme of such novels as Stephen King's *The Shining*, such movies as *House on Haunted Hill* (1959), and episodes of TV shows from *Thriller* to *Buffy the Vampire Slayer*. Not only is it one of the most prevalent tropes in horror, but it is also one of the oldest. Just as tales of ghosts go back in time immemorial, so too do tales of haunted houses.

Indeed, one of the earliest tales about a haunted house appears in a letter by Pliny the Younger written to his patron Lucias Sura. Pliny told the story of a house in Athens that had a bad reputation because no one could live there. In the dead of night there could be heard the clashing of iron and, if one listened closely, the rattling of chains. These noises would be followed by an apparition in the form of an old man with a long beard and messy hair, with chains on his feet and hands. Because of the ghost the house eventually became unoccupied, as people thought it was uninhabitable. When the philosopher Athenodorus came to Athens, he was drawn to this house by its exceedingly low rent. Athenodorus saw the ghost on his first night in the house, and followed the ghost to the courtyard where the spectre vanished. Athenodorus marked the spot where the ghost disappeared. He had the spot dug up where a skeleton in chains was discovered. The dead body of the old man was given a proper burial and the old man's ghost never bothered anyone again.

Another early tale of a haunted house is "Ali the Cairene and the Haunted House in Baghdad" from *One Thousand and One Nights*. "Ali the Cairene and the Haunted House in Baghdad" tells the story of a trader named Ali who visited Baghdad. In need of a place to stay, he asks about a particular house only to be told that the house is haunted by jinn and all who stay there die before the night's end. Despite the various warnings about the house, Ali decides to stay there anyway. He is indeed confronted by jinn that night, but instead of killing him the jinn give him copious amounts of gold.

The Icelandic saga *Eyrbyggja saga*, published in the 13th or 14th Century, contains several ghost stories, among which are some about haunted houses. The first concerned a rich, but not particularly healthy woman named Thorgunna. Upon her deathbed Thorgunna asked to be buried in Skálholt, for her sheets and bedding to be burned, and for all of her riches to be donated to the church. Unfortunately her friend Thorodd went against her wishes by giving her sheets to his wife as a gift. It was in the middle of the night that the men who had arrived to bear Thorgunna's corpse to Skálholt were awakened by a great clatter in the buttery. When they went to investigate they found Thorgunna there. They decided it was best to leave her to her own devices, and Thorgunna set about bringing food to the hall and setting the table. It was after Thoroddd had wished the men good cheer that Thorgunna left the hall and was never seen again. The men ate the food she had set out, with no harm to any of them. Thorgunna was buried in Skálholt.

Unfortunately Thorgunna would not be the last ghost to come haunting in *Eyrbyggja saga*. A shepherd who was an acquaintance of Thorgunna fell sick and died. It was not long afterwards that Thorir Wooden-leg encountered the shepherd's ghost. The shepherd's ghost assaulted him and Thorir fell sick and died. The shepherd and Thorir then began haunting the folk around the homestead of Frodis-water. Worse yet, six more people fell sick and died. The six dead men were often seen on a ten-oared boat not far from the shore. The ghosts grew even worse in their haunting during the Yule-feast. Finally Kiartan consulted Snorri the Priest as to what could be done about the ghosts. Snorri sent for another priest to accompany Kiartan to Frodis-water. The priest advised that Thorgunna's sheets be burned. Christian rituals were conducted afterwards among all the folk, and later the ghosts were put on trial for their wrongdoing. Once the ghosts were charged and sentenced they disappeared. Afterwards the priest spread holy water throughout the house. The folk at Frodis-water had no more problems with ghosts.

Haunted houses would later play a central role in Gothic literature. The first Gothic novel, *The Castle of Otranto* by Horace Wapole, featured many of the trappings of haunted house stories, including trapdoors, secret passages, doors that open and close by themselves, and so on. Indeed, *The Castle of Otranto* would not only have an impact on further Gothic novels, but on literature regarding haunted houses in general. The 19th Century would see some of the classics of the haunted house genre written. *The House of the Seven Gables* by Nathaniel Hawthorne drew heavily upon the mythos of haunted houses in a tale of an accursed house. Oscar Wilde's *The Canterville Ghost* took a more humorous look at haunted houses. Arguably *The Turn of the Screw* by Henry James is one of the archetypal haunted house tales. It centres upon a governess who may or may not have had an actual encounter with ghosts.

While one would think that stories of haunted houses would be old fashioned by the 20th Century, there would be several more classic novels on the subject, and haunted houses would provide fodder for many films during the century. Indeed, among the earliest such films was a silent comedy-drama simply titled *The Haunted House* (1912). Among the most influential haunted house movies was the black comedy *The Cat and the Canary* (1927), based on the 1922 comedy of the same name. It would be remade in 1939 starring Bob Hope and Paulette Goddard, although that version would be played even more for laughs. In the mid-20th Century haunted houses would nearly as often be grist for comedy as they would horror. There were such comedies as *The Ghost Breakers* (1940), *Hold That Ghost* (1941), and *Scared Stiff* (1953). Nearly every movie series, from the Mexican Sptifire to The Bowery Boys, had at least one entry set in a haunted house. That's not to say haunted houses weren't still ripe for horror movies. Such films as *The Uninvited* (1944), *House on Haunted Hill* (1959), *The Haunting* (1963), and *The Legend of Hell House* (1973) all utilised haunted houses as a source of terror.

Even given how ancient stories about haunted houses are, there were still many great haunted house tales published in the 20th Century. *The Haunting of Hill House* by Shirley Jackson became a classic in the genre and provided the basis for two movies titled *The Haunting*. *Hell House* by Robert Bloch would also prove to be one of the genre's classics. Stephen King's novel *The Shining* arguably established him as one of the top horror writers of the late 20th Century, and has been adapted both as a film and a mini-series.

Haunted houses would prove to be popular subjects for episodes of television shows. The classic horror anthology *Thriller* featured at least two episodes centred on haunted houses ("The Purple Room" and "What Beckoning Ghost?"). Sitcoms, including *The Andy Griffith Show* ("The Haunted House") and *The Monkees* ("Monkee See, Monkee Die"), touched upon the haunted house theme. Not surprisingly, horror series delved into haunted houses, including *Dark Shadows*, *Buffy the Vampire Slayer*, and *Angel*.

Given the popularity of haunted houses in literature, film, and television, it should perhaps not be surprising that there would develop the phenomenon of haunted attractions, whether actual houses reputed to be haunted or simulations thereof. One of the earliest haunted attractions was the Orton and Spooner Ghost House in Liphook, East Hampshire. It opened in 1915. The house still exists and is now part of the Hollycombe Steam Collection in Liphook.

It was in the late Fifties that haunted attractions took off in California. The San Mateo Haunted House opened in 1957 (sponsored by the Children's Health

Home Junior Auxiliary) and the San Bernardino Assistance League Haunted House opened in 1958. In the Sixties many haunted attractions opened in other parts of the United States. Among these was the Children's Museum Haunted House in Indianapolis. First opened in 1964, it has become the longest running "haunted house" in the United States. . The original Haunted Mansion ride was opened in Disneyland on August 9 1969, making haunted attractions even more popular across the nation. Since then there have evolved several variations on haunted attractions, from haunted trails to haunted hayrides. Haunted attractions have proven particularly popular with such organisations as the Jaycees and Kiwanis as fundraisers.

Tales of haunted houses go back centuries. It is a theme that has been repeated through many novels and movies for years. Despite this, there does not seem to be any indication that the haunted house will decline in popularity as a trope. Years from now there will probably still be books and movies coming out in which unsuspecting individuals find themselves face to face with ghosts (or simulations thereof) in some old, decrepit house.

Halloween at the Movies

To a large degree the rise in popularity of Halloween in the United States and the birth of cinema coincided with each other. The celebration of Halloween was brought to North America in the mid-19th Century by Scottish immigrants. By the 1880s and 1890s the celebration of Halloween had entered mainstream American society to the point that Halloween parties were not uncommon. English inventor Wordsworth Donisthorpe patented the first motion picture camera in 1876. Others would follow suit in the 1880s and 1890s. In 1893 the Edison Manufacturing Company showed the first kinetoscope film in public exhibition. The year 1895 arguably saw the birth of modern day cinema. That year Woodville Latham held the first commercial projection of a film in the United States and Auguste and Louis Lumière held the first commercial projection of a film in Europe. Given that the celebration of Halloween in the United States and motion pictures roughly grew up together, it should come as no surprise that Halloween would appear in movies from time to time in the early to mid-20th Century.

It is perhaps impossible to determine what the first film to reference Halloween was. That having been said, among the very earliest was the 1918 film *The Way of a Man with a Maid*. Directed by Donald Crisp and released by Paramount Pictures, the movie starred Bryant Washburn as a bookkeeper, Arthur McArney, trying to live on $21 a week. This is complicated when he falls in love with stenographer Elsa Owenson (played by Wanda Hawley), who has another suitor in the form of the wealthy Sankey (Jay Dwiggins). At one point in the film Arthur spends $200 in order to attend a swank Halloween party with Elsa. Unfortunately Arthur is called into work and Elsa attends the party with his rival Sankey.

Two films in 1934 would include Halloween in their plots. The first of these was *As the Earth Turns*, released by Warner Bros. and starring Jean Muir and Donald Woods. The film centres on a young couple struggling to make a living on a farm in Maine. Included in the film is a Halloween dance. The second film to mention Halloween released in 1934 was, of all things, a Western starring Ken Maynard, *Smoking Guns*. The plot involves Ken Masters (played by Ken Maynard) trying to clear his father of a crime. Included in the plot is a Halloween dance at which the villain plots to ambush Ken. Depending on when the film was set, it would seem to be a bit anachronistic. Halloween would not be widely celebrated in the United States until the 1880s, and Halloween parties would not become particularly common until the 1890s.

Halloween would play a more significant role in the 1937 movie *Boy of the Streets* starring Jackie Cooper. The film begins at Halloween in a slum in New York City. Children are dressed in costumes and going down the street on scooters, bicycles, and box cars. Many of them are pulling pranks, such as turning over trash cans. The film seems to acknowledge the Celtic roots of Halloween, as an Irish cop references having celebrated it in the Old Country. Here it must be pointed out that trick-or-treating does not play a role in the children's celebration of Halloween. Although the custom was already observed through parts of the United States, it had not quite yet spread to much of the East Coast.

Halloween also played a role in *Boy Friend* (1939), starring Jane Withers. In *Boy Friend* a police officer, Jimmy Murphy (played by Richard Bond), goes undercover as part of a gang. When one of the friends of his younger sister Sally (played by Miss Withers) is murdered, she and another one of her friends decide to solve the murder themselves. To this end she sneaks into the Golden Parrot Club, owned by mobsters, on Halloween and entertains the customers there, while her friend searches the basement.

Halloween would play a bigger role in the Ealing comedy *The Ghost of St. Michael's* (1941). The film starred Will Hay as a hapless teacher, William Lamb, who finds himself teaching at a school on the Isle of Skye and living in the haunted Dunbain Castle. During the film William catches the students celebrating "the feast of Halloween," which they describe as an old Scottish custom. Among other things, the students are stealing food and drink (including whiskey) for their party in their dorm. *The Ghost of St. Michael's* is notable as one of the earliest British films to reference Halloween.

The year 1944 would prove to be a significant one in the history of film with regards to Halloween, as two major releases (both now regarded as classics) dealt with the holiday. The first released of the two films was *Arsenic and Old Lace*, based on the hit Broadway play of the same name *Arsenic and Old Lace* was shot in 1941, but not released until 1944 after the play had ended its run. It stars Cary Grant as Mortimer Brewster, who visits his two spinster aunts (played by Josephine Hull and Jean Adair) upon the occasion of his marriage. Unfortunately for Mortimer, he soon learns that his aunts have a rather disturbing secret. Fittingly enough for a horror comedy, *Arsenic and Old Lace* is set entirely at Halloween. In fact, it quite possibly might be the first film to feature trick-or-treating. At one point in the film trick-or-treaters show up at the aunts' door and the aunts give them jack o' lanterns as treats. Of the films made during the Golden Age of Hollywood, perhaps no other movie has as strong a link to Halloween as *Arsenic and Old Lace* does, to the point that it would perhaps be accurate to say that it is to Halloween what *It's a Wonderful Life* (1946) or *Miracle on 34th Street* (1947) are to Christmas.

The second movie to be released in 1944 to deal with Halloween was *Meet Me in St. Louis*, which was based on Sally Benson's book of the same name, a novel that grew out of her short stories originally published as a series in *The New Yorker* under the title "5135 Kensington". *Meet Me in St. Louis* followed the lives of the Smith family in St. Louis during the year leading up to the World's Fair (1903-1904). A rather long segment of *Meet Me in St. Louis* is set at Halloween in 1903, and is particularly interesting for its portrayal of Halloween customs at the start of the 20th Century. The segment begins with youngest Smith daughters Tootie (played by Margaret O'Brien) and Agnes (Joan Carroll) getting dressed in their costumes for Halloween. Tootie goes to the door of a dreaded neighbour, Mr. Braukoff (played by Mayo Newhall), and throws flour on him (believe it or not, this was a common Halloween prank at the turn of the 20th Century). Later Tootie and Agnes are nearly killed when they try the rather dangerous prank of placing a dummy on the trolley tracks.

The following year, 1945, saw the release of another film that included Halloween, *The Woman Who Came Back*. It was one of the very few horror films of the era to acknowledge the holiday. *The Woman Who Came Back* centred on Lorna Webster (played by Nancy Kelly), who returns to her hometown in New England. Descended from the witch hunter Elijah Webster, she soon becomes convinced that she is possessed by a famous witch from the past. Fittingly enough, Lorna arrives in her hometown on Halloween. Halloween decorations adorn the houses in the town, and children are wearing their Halloween costumes.

While Halloween played fairly significant roles in *Arsenic and Old Lace*, *Meet Me in St. Louis*, and *The Woman Who Came Back*, it played only a minor role in *My Blue Heaven* (1950). *My Blue Heaven* centred on Kitty and Jack Moran (played by Betty Grable and Dan Dailey), a married song and dance team who want to adopt a child. As might be expected of a Betty Grable musical, it features several song and dance numbers. Among the numbers is one dedicated to Halloween, complete with a jab at Irving Berlin for having written songs for every single holiday except it.

Despite its title, Halloween would play a major role in the 1960 Hayley Mills movie *Summer Magic*. Indeed, the movie climaxes with a house warming party held on Halloween. Quite naturally, the party has many of the trappings of the holiday, including jack o' lanterns and corn shocks.

Halloween would also play a role in the film *Conrack* (1974). *Conrack* starred Jon Voight as Pat Conroy, a young teacher assigned to Yamacraw Island off the coast of South Carolina. As it turns out Yamacraw Island is extremely isolated. In fact, most of the residents speak a dialect of Gulah. Conroy strives to teach his students about the outside world. To this end he takes his students to Beaufort on the mainland for Halloween, an excursion that would mark their first significant interaction with the outside world. This does not sit well with the school's superintendent, Mr. Skeffington (played by Hume Cronyn), who takes Conroy to task for it.

The year 1976 would prove to be a fruitful one for films referencing Halloween, with no less than three movies released. *The Little Girl Who Lives Down the Lane* (1976) begins at Halloween, which also happens to be the birthday of the main character Rynn Jacobs (played by Jodie Foster). The movie features children in costume trick-or-treating. Rynn, who is from England, knows very little about Halloween and has to have the holiday explained to her.

Prior to the Eighties it was a rare thing for horror movies to be set at Halloween. An exception to this rule was *The Clown Murders* (1976). In an effort to spoil a businessman's real estate deal, four friends dress up as clowns on Halloween and kidnap his wife. Unfortunately, the four friends find themselves hunted by a killer in a clown costume. While not a very good film, *The Clown Murders* is significant as one of the earliest films to deal with the now common "evil clown" trope.

Kenny & Company (1976) was a much more innocent film than the thriller *The Little Girl Who Lives Down the Lane* or *The Clown Murders*. It followed the three days leading up to Halloween in the life of a boy named Kenny (played by Dan McCann). *Kenny & Company* captures Halloween as it was observed by boys in the Seventies very well. Halloween is a bit in the background in the early part of the film, although Kenny and his friends are making their plans for it. They are getting their costumes ready and determining the best houses to visit. The climax of *Kenny & Company* takes place on Halloween, with the boys trick-or-treating and Kenny being sent into a scary looking house.

It would be in 1978 that a film would be released that would change things forever. Aside from *Arsenic and Old Lace* and *Meet Me in St. Louis*, John Carpenter's *Halloween* may be the most famous movie to deal with the holiday. As its name suggests, the film takes place almost entirely on Halloween. The film centres on Laurie (played by Jamie Lee Curtis), a babysitter who finds herself facing the psychotic killer Michael Meyers. As might be expected *Halloween* featured some of the trappings of the holiday, including brief sightings of trick-or-treaters and jack o' lanterns.

Halloween would prove to be a smash hit at the box office. It would also have a lasting influence. While it was not the first slasher movie, the success of

Halloween would spur a cycle towards slasher films that would last well into the Eighties. And while only a few horror movies were set at Halloween prior to the release of *Halloween*, afterwards there would be a whole slough of horror movies set, at least in part, on the holiday. Among these films were *The Amityville Horror* (1979), *The Changeling* (1980), *Creepshow* (1982) *Trick or Treat* (1986), and *Demonic Toys* (1992).

In addition to feature films, Halloween would also prove to be a popular theme for theatrical animated shorts. Most series had at least one Halloween entry. "Felix the Cat Switches Witches" (1927) pitted Felix against witches at Halloween. The title of "Betty Boop's Hallowe'en Party" (1933) is pretty much self-explanatory. "Trick or Treat" (1952) is considered one of the all-time classic Donald Duck shorts, featuring Huey, Duey, and Louie and Disney's version of Witch Hazel. "Broom-Stick Bunny" (1956) pitted Bugs Bunny against Warner Bros.' version of Witch Hazel on Halloween.

With regards to live-action short subjects, the classic "Our Gang" short "Bouncing Babies" is set at Halloween and features the gang in costumes. It also features Halloween pranks, including one in which the gang changes Wheezer's little brother with a goat.

Halloween celebrations in the United States grew up alongside the cinema. Ultimately motion pictures would chronicle many of the changes to the holiday over the years. Early films centred primarily on Halloween parties. Halloween pranks made their appearance in sound films fairly early. *Arsenic and*

Old Lace marked what might be the first instance of trick-or-treating on film, a custom that would be featured in many movies set at Halloween to come. And while horror movies of the Golden Age were rarely set at Halloween eventually it would become commonplace for horror films to be set on the holiday following the release of *Halloween*. The celebration of Halloween in the United States and motion pictures emerged at about the same time, and it seems likely that they will continue to evolve together.

Orson Welles's *War of the Worlds* Radio Broadcast

The *War of the Worlds* broadcast *of The Mercury Theatre of the Air*, produced by Orson Welles, is quite possibly the most famous single broadcast of a radio programme of all time. Sadly, it is not famous for its high quality (although it is one of the greatest episodes of a radio show ever) or because it won awards (it didn't), but rather it is famous for the panic it was alleged to have caused across the United States. Quite simply, many people across the nation may have been convinced Martians were invading Earth. It aired on October 30 1938, just in time for Halloween. At the end of the broadcast Orson Welles assured everyone, that it was "Mercury Theatre's own radio version of dressing up in a sheet and jumping out of a bush and saying Boo!"

The Mercury Theatre of the Air debuted on CBS in July of 1938. It brought John Houseman and Orson Welles's Mercury Theatre to radio. Its concept was simple, but unique in radio at the time--to bring classic material (books, plays, et. al.) to the air, performed by the Mercury Theatre troupe. The show had debuted with a performance of the novel *Dracula* and over the course of the next few weeks would adapt *Treasure Island*, *A Tale of Two Cities*, *The Count of Monte Cristo*, and other classics to radio. For their Halloween episode, the Mercury Theatre settled upon H. G. Wells' *War of the Worlds*. Howard Koch's script moved the classic novella's action from

Victorian London to the United States in 1938. Indeed, the Martians would begin their invasion in Grover Mills, New Jersey.

 The script, officially titled "The Invasion from Mars," took a relatively unique approach in American radio at the time in that it played out as a series of newscasts reporting an invasion of Earth by Martian tripods. Although it was the first time an episode of a dramatic radio show took this form in the United States, such an approach had been taken before. In 1926 Monsignor Ronald Knox produced a satirical radio show in the form of a newscast of a riot in London. Broadcast over the BBC, this radio show also caused a bit of a panic in London.

It is perhaps for this reason that "The Invasion from Mars" included a disclaimer at the start of the programme, its middle, and at its end, along with many spread through the show created by local CBS affiliates around the country, stating categorically that it was simply a fictional radio drama. The show was announced in newspaper radio listings ahead of the fact of the broadcast. Even in the broadcast itself the year was given as 1939, a clear sign this was not an actual newscast (it was 1938, after all). Despite this, there were people who, at least for a time, honestly believed that Earth was being invaded by Mars.

The precise scale of the panic caused by Orson Welles' broadcast of "The Invasion from Mars" is difficult to judge today. That there was a panic there can be no doubt. The switchboards at CBS were jammed with calls from people concerned about the invasion. *The New York Times* itself would receive

832 calls. A month after the broadcast there had been an estimated 12,500 newspaper stories on the broadcast according to Professor Ronald Hand in the book *Terror on the Air!: Horror Radio in America, 1931-1952* (including *The New York Times*, who featured it as the headlining story on their front page). Immediately following the end of the broadcast of "The Invasion from Mars," police arrived at the CBS studio in New York. They took both John Houseman and Orson Welles to one of the CBS offices for questioning. Neither man was ever arrested. After the police released Houseman and Welles, they faced a rather hostile crowd of reporters. They would eventually have to sneak out of the building through the back door to make it to a rehearsal of *Danton's Death*. The next morning CBS held a press conference where Orson Welles read what was a combination disclaimer and apology. The press conference was filmed for newsreels across the country.

While it is obvious that there was a panic, it is questionable if it was as large as the press made it out to be at the time. Stanley J. Baran and Dennis K. Davis in *Mass Communication Theory: Foundations, Ferment, and Future* make the suggestion that the scale of the panic was not as large as newspapers at the time made it out to be. They point out that many in the newspaper industry saw radio as a competitor and worried that the relatively new medium would put newspapers out of business. As a result, they were largely unsympathetic to CBS, John Houseman, and Orson Welles. It must be pointed out that in the Thirties; yellow journalism still persisted on a widespread scale in the press in the United States.

Because of this many newspapers simply avoided the facts and took the chance to prove that radio could be a dangerous medium by exaggerating the overall scale of the panic. In their book *Panic Attacks*, Robert Bartholomew and Hilary Evans believe that thousands of people were indeed frightened for a time, but that ultimately reports of individuals acting on their fear of an invasion from Mars is both "scant" and "anecdotal." Indeed, it seems that while many people in many locations did call the police about the invasion, there is little evidence to suggest that they did anything more than call the police.

As to what ultimately caused the panic, that remains a question to this day. The broadcast is in many respects very convincing and could perhaps be taken as an actual newscast by the casual listener. In fact, it was on October 30 1938 that we have some of the earliest evidence for the phenomenon then called "zapping" and now known as "channel surfing." Quite simply, as was typical on a Sunday night in 1938, many were listening to *The Chase and Sanborn Hour* (so named because it was sponsored by Chase and Sanborn Coffee) starring ventriloquist Edgar Bergen and his dummy Charlie McCarthy on NBC Red. It was around fifteen minutes into *The Chase and Sanborn Hour* that the first comedy sketch with Edgar Bergen ended. With the start of a musical segment, many switched from NBC Red to CBS. For that reason they missed the first announcement that the broadcast was not a real newscast, but merely a dramatisation. Despite this, a lack of knowledge cannot be entirely credited with causing the panic. It must be pointed out that this was the first time in the United States that a dramatic radio show took the form of a newscast. The average radio listener was then simply not used to newsflashes being used for dramatic effect.

This was compounded by the fact that in the Northeast, at least, individuals would visit their neighbours to ask what was happening. As a result stories of the invasion from Mars would be repeated and would start to take shape as rumours, which would then spread making the panic all the worse. Some persist as urban legends to this day. It must also be pointed out that at the time World War II was already brewing in Europe and many Americans had very real anxieties as to an oncoming war. "The Invasion of Mars" perhaps fed into these anxieties, which may have made individuals more inclined to believe that Martians were invading Earth. Of course, critic for *The New Yorker* and radio personality Alexander Woollcott had a different theory on the cause of the panic. The next day he sent Welles a telegram which simply read, "This only goes to prove, my beamish boy, that the intelligent people were all listening to a dummy, and all the dummies were listening to you." Orson Welles would post the telegram on the door to his office.

While the exact causes of the panic which ensued following the *War of the Worlds* broadcast may never be known, it did have some very real consequences. Sadly for CBS, Orson Welles's lawyer, Arnold Weissberger, had written into his contract that the network, not Welles, would be held responsible for anything questionable Welles did on *The Mercury Theatre of the Air*. There were threats of lawsuits in the wake of the broadcast. CBS may well have won every case, given that the programme had been announced ahead of time in newspapers and the three disclaimers that aired on the show itself. Even if CBS had lost every case, they were hardly hurting from money because of "The Invasion from Mars." The Campbell Soup Company, which had previously turned down sponsorship of *The Mercury Theatre of the Air*, volunteered to be the show's sponsor following the broadcast. The listenership of the show also jumped nearly 100% following the airing of "The Invasion of Mars."

While CBS may have been relatively unharmed by lawsuits, they would be hurt in other ways. Following an investigation into the matter, the Federal Communications Commission called CBS into account for failing to monitor their broadcasts for the incident. Since the time of the *War of the Worlds* broadcast, both radio and television networks have made sure during any dramatic broadcast taking the form of a newscast to have plentiful disclaimers that it is simply a fictional programme. During both the telefilm *Special Bulletin* in 1983 and the 1994 telefilm, *Without Warning* in 1994, which took the form of newscasts, many disclaimers telling viewers that this was a fictional account were aired.

In the years since it first aired, Orson Welles's *War of the Worlds* broadcast has become legendary. It has been remade several times, including by Buffalo radio station WKBW in 1968 (who updated it again), Denver station KHOW in 1987, and Washington, D.C. station WBIG-FM in 1997 (which also updated it). On October 30 1988, the 50th anniversary of the broadcast, PBS aired its own remake. The first dramatisation of the panic itself, "The Night America Trembled," appeared on *Studio One* in 1957. In 1975 ABC would air a TV movie based on the panic, *The Night That Panicked America*. There have been many pop culture references to the *War of the Worlds* broadcast, from the novel version of *2001: a Space Odyssey* to the movie *The Adventures of Buckaroo Banzai Across the 8th Dimension* to an episode of the TV series *War of the Worlds* scheduled to coincide with the broadcast's 50th anniversary (on which it was explained that the United States government paid Orson Welles to make the broadcast to cover up a Martian reconnaissance mission--the Martians would begin on all out invasion in 1953, fifteen years later, when the movie version of *War of the Worlds* was released).

While it is best known for the panic it inspired, the lasting influence of "The Invasion from Mars" is probably not due to that notoriety, but due to the fact that it is a very good radio show. "The Invasion from Mars" has been widely available since the Sixties. It is to be found on both CDs and in MP3 format today. "The Invasion from Mars" is very convincing. That having been said, it is also very dramatic and entertaining--one of the best radio shows I have ever heard. If it is still remembered today, then much of it is due to the quality of "The Invasion of the Mars" as it is the panic it inspired.

Arsenic and Old Lace

Frank Capra apparently had a knack for making films that would be forever linked to specific holidays. *It's a Wonderful Life* (1946) is a perennial Yuletide favourite. *Meet John Doe* (1941) is also linked to that particular holiday. As to Frank Capra's adaptation of *Arsenic and Old Lace* (1944), it has always been tied to Halloween. There should be little wonder that it is. Not only is *Arsenic and Old Lace* set at Halloween, but its subject matter makes it perfect viewing for the holiday.

Arsenic and Old Lace centres on drama critic Mortimer Brewster (Cary Grant), who returns to visit his spinster aunts, Martha (Jean Adair) and Abbey (Josephine Hull) following his wedding. His cousin Teddy (John Alexander), who lives with his two aunts, believes that he is Teddy Roosevelt. When Mortimer discovers a dead body in a window seat, he concludes that Teddy must have committed murder. It is not long before Mortimer learns the shocking truth behind the murder. Worse yet, his homicidal brother Jonathan (Raymond Massey) shows up. Jonathan brings with him surgeon Dr. Einstein (Peter Lorre), with the plan that Einstein will perform plastic surgery on him so he won't be recognisable to the police As might be expected, hardly anything goes according to plan for either Mortimer or Jonathan.

The film *Arsenic and Old Lace* was based on the hit Broadway play of the same name by Joseph Kesselring, who wrote it in 1939. As hard as it is to believe, the black comedy had some basis in real life.

It is commonly believed at Bethel College in North Newton, Kansas that Goerz House at the college served as the basis for the Brewster sisters' home. While Mr. Kesserling taught at the college he lived at Goerz House, which at the time served as both a residence for male teachers and a men's dormitory. Among its features were a rather large window seat and a cellar with a dirt floor, much like the Brewsters' house. At Bethel College it is also believed that the Brewster sisters themselves might have been based on people he met while living in Kansas.

Of course, no murders were ever committed at Goerz House at Bethel College. That having been said, the inspiration for that part of the plot of *Arsenic and Old Lace* might have been based on a real life murder case. Amy Archer-Gilligan was the owner of a nursing home, the Archer Home for the Elderly and Infirm in Windsor, Connecticut. For lifetime care at the nursing home, one only needed to pay Archer-Gilligan a one-time fee of $1000. Unfortunately, she had a novel means of making more room at the home and thus creating more business. Quite simply, between 1907 and 1917 Archer-Gilligan murdered several of the residents at her nursing home for their pension money. She was charged with five counts of murder, which her lawyer got reduced to one count, although she might have been guilty of many more (between 1907 and 1917 there were sixty deaths at the nursing home). As to how she committed the murders, Archer-Gilligan had been buying arsenic in bulk, ostensibly to deal with a rat problem.

Prior to *Arsenic and Old Lace* Joseph Kesserling had not been particularly successful as a playwright. His first play on Broadway, *There's Wisdom in Women*, closed after only 46 performances in 1935. His third play, *Cross-town*, did even worse. It closed after only five performances in 1937. Fortunately Mr. Kesserling sent a copy of *Arsenic and Old Lace* (then titled *Bodies in Our Cellar*) to actress Dorothy Stickney with the idea that she could play one of the aunts. Ultimately she would not, but Miss Stickney was married to Howard Lindsay, who with Russel Crouse formed a successful writing team on Broadway. Mr. Lindsay saw potential in the script for *Bodies in Our Cellar* and as a result Lindsay and Crouse decided to make the play their first joint production on Broadway. Allegedly Lindsay and Crouse rewrote the play a good deal, although they took no credit for it publicly.

To direct *Arsenic and Old Lace* (as the play was retitled), Lindsay and Crouse turned to Bretaigne Windust, who had directed Lindsay and Crouse's hit play *Life with Father* in 1939. For the important role of serial killer Jonathan Brewster, Lindsay and Crouse recruited Boris Karloff (the line "He looks like Boris Karloff!" was then an in-joke that got uproarious laughter from audiences when the play was first performed on Broadway). For the other roles in the play Lindsay and Crouse hired Broadway veterans: Josephine Hull; Jean Adair; John Alexander; Allyn Joslyn; and Edgar Stehli.

The play *Arsenic and Old Lace* made its debut in a trial run in Baltimore, Maryland on December 26 1940. The show opened to overwhelmingly positive notices from critics. It also proved to be a smash hit. It was then on January 10 1941 that *Arsenic and Old*

Lace made its debut on Broadway at the Fulton
Theatre (now called the Helen Hayes Theatre). It
proved to be an enormous success. As in Baltimore
the reviews from critics were overwhelmingly
positive. What is more, *Arsenic and Old Lace* was
playing to largely full houses. The play would remain
at the Fulton Theatre until September 25 1943,
whereupon it moved to the Hudson Theatre. It was
there that it closed on June 17 1944 after 1,444
performances.

Such success did not go unnoticed by Hollywood.
Nearly every major studio sought the film rights to
Arsenic and Old Lace, including Paramount and
Samuel Goldwyn. In the end it was Warner Bros. who
won the rights to the play, closing the deal less than a
month after *Arsenic and Old Lace* had opened on
Broadway. As part of the deal Lindsay and Crouse
insisted that the film could not open until January 1
1943, giving the play a chance to run two years on
Broadway. As it was the play would run considerably
longer and in the end the film would not be released
until September 23 1944.

Lindsay and Crouse were hoping that René Clair
would direct the film version of *Arsenic and Old
Lace*. Instead Jack L. Warner chose Frank Capra, who
had directed such hit films as *It Happened One Night*
(1934), *You Can't Take It With You* (1938), and *Mr.
Smith Goes to Washington* (1939). The screenplay
was written by Julius J. Epstein and Philip G. Epstein.
The screenplay would depart from the play in some
respects, largely because of the Production Code. The
line, "I'm not a Brewster! I'm a bastard!" had to be
altered in order to conform to the Code. Another

change made in the film is that in the play Mortimer and Elaine are only engaged, while in the film they have just married. Yet another change made for the film is that while the play is set in September, the film is set on Halloween.

The casting of the lead role of Mortimer for the film version of *Arsenic and Old Lace* would take some time. Originally Warner Bros. wanted Bob Hope for the role. Although it might seem odd now, there's no doubt that it made perfect sense to Warner Bros. at the time. Bob Hope had recently starred in two hit horror comedies for Paramount: *The Cat and the Canary* (1939) and *The Ghost Breakers* (1940), which they probably thought made him a good choice for *Arsenic and Old Lace*, yet another horror comedy. Unfortunately for Warner Bros., Bob Hope was under contract to Paramount and that studio refused to loan him out. Reportedly Frank Capra offered the role to Jack Benny, who was then under contract to Warner Bros., but Jack Benny turned him down. On August 11 1941 Warner Bros. announced that Richard Travis (now best known as Bertram H. Jefferson in *The Man Who Came to Dinner*) would play Mortimer. This changed on September 30 1941 when Warner Bros. announced that Cary Grant had been cast in the role.

The role of Mortimer would not be the only one that would prove difficult to cast. The role of Jonathan would as well. Warner Bros. wanted Boris Karloff to play the role, but Lindsay and Crouse did not want to release him from the play for two months to make the film. They tried to convince Warner Bros. to wait until June 1942, when Boris Karloff (and the rest of the cast, for that matter) would be free to do the film.

Lindsay and Crouse believed that Boris Karloff was the play's chief asset and without him ticket sales could actually go down. Ultimately Raymond Massey would be cast in the role of homicidal sociopath Jonathan Brewster.

Then as now Raymond Massey was best known for playing villains in such films as *The Prisoner of Zenda* (1937) and *Santa Fe Trail* (1940). He had appeared with Boris Karloff in *The Old Dark House* (1932). He also resembled Boris Karloff insofar as both men were tall and somewhat menacing in appearance. As it was Frank Capra insisted that make up be used to make Raymond Massey look even more like Boris Karloff. This alarmed Warner's legal department, who had Mr. Karloff sign a release so that he would not sue the studio.

While Boris Karloff did not get to appear in the film version of *Arsenic and Old Lace*, his co-stars from the play Josephine Hull, Jean Adair, and John Alexander were able to recreate their respective roles of Aunt Abby, Aunt Martha, and Cousin Teddy for the film. The three actors were given eight weeks off from the play in order to play their parts in the film. Their roles were taken over by Patricia Collinge, Minnie Dupree, and Harry Gribbon respectively.

For the most part the rest of the cast was filled out by players under contract to Warner Bros. Legendary actor Peter Lorre played the role of plastic surgeon Dr. Einstein. Priscilla Lane played Mortimer's new wife, Elaine. Jack Carson played the rather clueless Officer O'Hara. Legendary character actor Edward Everett Horton was one of the exceptions in the cast.

He spent nearly his entire career as a freelancer, so he was not under contract to Warner Bros. when he played Mr. Witherspoon, the superintendent of Happy Dale Sanitarium.

For its adaptation of *Arsenic and Old Lace* Warner Bros. spared no expense. Its cinematographer would be Sol Polito, who had already shot such classic films as *I Am a Fugitive from a Chain Gang* (1932), *42nd Street* (1933), *The Adventures of Robin Hood* (1938), and *Angels with Dirty Faces* (1938). He had already been nominated for one Academy Award, for his photography on *The Private Lives of Elizabeth and Essex* (1939). Max Steiner, then as now known for his work on *King Kong* and *Gone with the Wind,* would compose the score. *Arsenic and Old Lace* was budgeted at $1,220,000 then a respectable sum for a film. It was given a shooting schedule of 48 days or, more simply, eight weeks.

Arsenic and Old Lace was shot from October 20 1941 to December 16 1941. Despite this it would be some time before the movie would be seen by audiences in the United States. As mentioned earlier, Lindsay and Crouse did not want the film released while *Arsenic and Old Lace* was still playing on Broadway. Initially they had thought the play would have ended its run by January 1 1943 at the latest. As it turned out *Arsenic and Old Lace* was such a roaring success that it ran until June 17 1944. While Warner Bros. would not release the film during this time, it was shown to troops serving overseas in World War II during 1943.

It was also during this period that the film would undergo one change from its original, completed version. The original, completed version of the movie *Arsenic and Old Lace* ended with Aunts Abby and Martha poisoning one last victim, Mr. Witherspoon. The Breen Office was none too happy with this ending, and it turned out that preview audiences were not either. In the end Warner Bros. simply cut the ending off, so the film ends with Mortimer, Elaine, and the taxi driver in the cemetery.

With the play's Broadway run completed *Arsenic and Old Lace* premiered at the Strand in New York City on September 1 1944. It went into general release on September 23 1944. In the intervening time two of the film's cast members had died: Edward McWade, who played the murder victim Gibbs, and Spencer Charters, who played the Marriage Licence Clerk. Priscilla Lane was also no longer with Warner Bros., the actress and the studio having terminated her contract by mutual consent not long after *Arsenic and Old Lace* had finished shooting.

The film *Arsenic and Old Lace* would prove very successful. It would literally play for weeks in several cities. Ultimately the film made $2,836,000 in the United States and $1,948,000 overseas. The film also received largely positive reviews. Donald Kirkley wrote in the *Baltimore Sun*, "The epic, macabre humour of *Arsenic and Old Lace* has been fully retained in the screen version... In some ways the film is superior." *The New York Times* reviewer wrote of the film, "Frank Capra has put into the picture all of the riotous farce, gentle naiveté and broad melodrama that Messrs. Howard Lindsay and Russel Crouse put originally into the Joseph Kesselring stage play."

Curiously not everyone was happy with the film adaptation of *Arsenic and Old Lace*. Cary Grant felt that he overplayed Mortimer Brewster and that Allyn Joslyn (who originated the role on stage) was much better. He also felt Jimmy Stewart would have done a better job of playing Mortimer in the film. Mr. Grant considered *Arsenic and Old Lace* to be his least favourite performance on film.

It would appear that audiences have disagreed with Cary Grant over the years. *Arsenic and Old Lace* continued to do brisk business well into 1945. The film would later prove to be a favourite on television, where it is among Frank Capra's most frequently shown films. Indeed, for many television stations airing *Arsenic and Old Lace* is a Halloween tradition.

As a postscript it must be noted that while Boris Karloff did not get to play Jonathan Brewster on film, he did eventually get to play the role in a television adaptation of the play. On January 5 1955 the CBS series *The Best of Broadway* aired an adaptation of the play that not only featured Boris Karloff as Jonathan Brewster, but John Alexander as Cousin Teddy, Peter Lorre as Dr. Einstein, and Edward Everett Horton as Mr. Witherspoon. Josephine Hull would go from *Arsenic and Old Lace* to another great success on Broadway, the play *Harvey*. She would reprise her role as Veta Louise Simmons in the 1950 film version of *Harvey* as well.

Over seventy years after its release *Arsenic and Old Lace* not only remains popular, but also well respected. At film review site Rotten Tomatoes the film has a rather phenomenal rating of 92%. At

IMDB it has a rating of 8.1 out of 10. In 2000 the American Film Institute placed *Arsenic and Old Lace* at #30 in its "100 Years...100 Laughs" list of the funniest movies of all time. Originating as a smash hit Broadway play, *Arsenic and Old Lace* has gone on to become one of the best loved film comedies of all time.

Halloween on Television: 1952-1982

Halloween episodes of television shows have a long history going back to the Fifties. To a large degree this can be traced back to radio, where a lot of the old radio shows also had Halloween episodes. *The Jack Benny Program*, *The Baby Snooks Show*, *Father Knows Best*, and many other radio programmes did Halloween episodes. Indeed, the most famous Halloween episode of all time may not belong to a television show, but to a radio show instead. The October 30 1938 *War of the Worlds* broadcast of *The Mercury Theatre* remains remembered to this day.

Given the popularity of Halloween episodes on radio, it should be little wonder that many television shows would follow suit with their own Halloween episodes. Airing in October or, at the latest, on November 1, these episodes did not always have Halloween as a theme. Some shows simply elected for episodes about haunted houses, ghosts, or other spooky subject matter suitable to the holiday. Regardless, since the Sixties viewers have been able to look forward to special Halloween episodes of their favourite shows every October.

Regularly scheduled network television broadcasts began in the United States in 1946. Given the nature of these early broadcasts, it would be difficult to say with any certainty what the very first Halloween episode of a television show was. Certainly one of the earliest was "Halloween Party", an episode of *The*

Adventures of Ozzie and Harriet that aired on Halloween in 1952. Ozzie and Harriet Nelson had also done a Halloween episode on their radio show. In "Halloween Party" Ozzie and his friend Thorny (Don DeFore) plan a Halloween party. Being *The Adventures of Ozzie and Harriet*, naturally it does not go as planned.

The Honeymooners would spend only one season as its own show, existing for most of its history as a series of sketches on *The Jackie Gleason Show*. It was on *The Jackie Gleason Show* that *The Honeymooners* first dealt with Halloween. "Question Mark" (also known as "Masquerade" and "Halloween Party") aired on the October 25 1952 episode of *The Jackie Gleason Show* and featured the Kramdens and Nortons dressing up in costume for a Halloween party. Another Halloween themed *Honeymooners* sketch would air the following year. On "Halloween Party" Ralph ruins the tuxedo he planned to wear for the bus company's Halloween party, not realising it is not a costume party anyway.

When the subject of Halloween comes up, the TV show *Lassie* is probably not the first television programme to come mind. That having been said, *Lassie* featured two Halloween themed episodes in the Fifties. "The Witch" aired on October 30 1955. On the show Jeff (played by Tommy Rettig) and Porky (played by Donald Keeler) are convinced that an eccentric old lady is a witch. Halloween plays a role in the *Lassie* episode "Trapped", which aired on October 26 1958. In the episode Timmy (played by Jon Provost) and Boomer (played by Todd Ferrell) are searching for foxfire to smear on their faces for a

Halloween party when they fall through the floor of an old house and become trapped there. *Lassie* would have one last Halloween episode late in its run. "Wings of the Ghost" aired in syndication around October 28 1971. In the episode Lassie, Ron (played by Robert Burton), and Dale (played by Larry Wilcox) stay in a barn that may be haunted.

Being set in California in the early 19th Century where Halloween was unknown, the TV series *Zorro* never dealt with the holiday itself, but it had a Halloween episode nonetheless. "The Ghost of the Mission" aired on Halloween in 1957. In the episode Capt. Monastario plots to take over a mission that is rumoured to be haunted. To thwart Monastario's plans, Zorro comes up with his own plan: convincing Monastario's men that the mission's ghost is real.

The Phil Silvers Show episode "Bilko's Vampire" aired on October 1 1958, but given its subject matter and its relative proximity to the holiday, it could be considered a Halloween episode. In the episode Sgt. Ritzik (played by Joe E. Ross) not only becomes addicted to watching old horror movies on television, but eventually becomes convinced that he is a vampire as well.

While Halloween episodes of TV shows were not particularly common in the Fifties, they would become much, much more prevalent during the Sixties. In fact, during many seasons there might be several different Halloween episodes on various shows. With the 1961-1962 season there would be Halloween episodes of two classic sitcoms. The *Donna Reed Show* episode "The Monster" aired on

October 12 1961. When the family discover tracks belonging to a large animal and keep hearing noises during the night, they become convinced some sort of monster is about. In the *Dennis the Menace* episode "Haunted House", which aired on October 29 1961, Dennis's father Henry and their neighbour Mr. Wilson buy a house only to learn that it is allegedly haunted.

If there was ever a banner year for Halloween episodes on television, it might well have been 1962. The 1962-1963 season would feature more Halloween episodes of TV shows than many previous seasons combined. What is more, it was not simply sitcoms in 1962 that featured Halloween episodes, but dramas as well. Some of the Halloween episodes airing in 1962 are now regarded as among the very best.

What might have been the earliest Halloween episode to air in the 1962-1963 season was "Haunted House", the October 7 1962 episode of *The Andy Griffith Show*. The episode begins when Opie (played by Ron Howard) and his friend Arnold (played by Ronnie Dapo) accidentally hit a baseball into a house they think is haunted. They are too scared to retrieve it. Barney (played by Don Knotts) thinks Andy (played by Andy Griffith) should make the boys get the baseball themselves, but is no braver than the boys when it comes to getting the ball back. As it turns out, while there are some strange goings on in the house, everything is not as it seems.

The *My Three Sons* episode "The Ghost Next Door", which aired on October 25 1962 , is set on Halloween and even features Chip (played by Stanley Livingston) and his friend Sudsy (played by Ricky

Allen) trick-or-treating. Of course, while doing so they notice someone carrying a candle in the house next door. While they are convinced it was a ghost, no one else believes them.

The following night, October 26 1962, there aired one of the Halloween episodes on a drama that season. The *Route 66* episode "Lizard's Leg and Owlet's Wing" reunited horror stars Boris Karloff, Lon Chaney Jr., and Peter Lorre, who play themselves in the episode. The three masters of horror have met to debate whether the old horrors are still scary at a hotel at which Tod (played by Martin Milner) and Buz (played by George Maharis) are working. It would be the last time that Boris Karloff would appear in the classic Frankenstein's monster makeup and the last time Lon Chaney Jr. appeared in the Wolfman makeup.

What was the number one show of the 1962-1963 season was a brand new show, *The Beverly Hillbillies*. Its very first season it featured a Halloween episode, "Trick or Treat". Granny (played by Irene Ryan) is missing the hills and complaining that none of their neighbours in Beverly Hills come to visit the way they did back home. Jed (played by Buddy Ebsen) suggests to Granny that they visit their neighbours. Of course, it just happens to be Halloween. The episode is historic as it features the first reference to Hooterville, later the setting of fellow sitcoms *Petticoat Junction* and *Green Acres*. Of course, here it must be pointed out that given the number of Scots who settled the hills in the South (and the Scots having brought Halloween to America), chances are good that the Clampetts would be familiar with Halloween. That having been said, as in the episode, they probably would not be familiar with trick-or-treating, which only came about in the 20th Century.

The Beverly Hillbillies would have only one other Halloween episode. "The Ghost of Clampett Castle" was part of a story arc in which the Clampetts inherited an English castle and visited England. In the episode, in an effort to get them to go back to California, Mr. Drysdale (played by Raymond Bailey) makes up a story about the ghost of Lady Clementine, whose husband was murdered in the castle by her own grandmother and tells it to Granny. "The Ghost of Clampett Castle" aired on October 23 1968.

The final Halloween episode of the 1962-1963 season actually aired on November 1 1962, All Saints' Day. The *Perry Mason* episode "The Case of the Dodging Domino" begins with a murder on Halloween and trick-or-treating actually plays a pivotal role in the plot.

The TV show that might be the all-time champion when it comes to Halloween episodes debuted in the 1964-1965 season. Of course, given *Bewitched* was about a witch (Samantha, played by Elizabeth Montgomery) who married a mortal (Darrin, played by Dick York for most of its run and Dick Sargent later on), it should perhaps not be surprising that the show would feature several Halloween episodes. Indeed, for a time the show did one Halloween episode a year.

The first of the Halloween episodes of *Bewitched* was "The Witches Are Out", which aired on October 29

1964. In "The Witches Are Out" Darrin, at his advertising agency, creates a Halloween campaign featuring a witch as an old crone. Samantha and her relatives take offence and accuse Darrin of stereotyping witches. The episode is notable as featuring the first appearance of Aunt Clara (played by Marion Lorne), who would become one of the show's most prominent characters. The next year's Halloween episode, "Trick or Treat", would also deal with the stereotyping of witches. Darrin's boss Larry Tate (played by David White) sends Samantha some typical Halloween decorations for their small, Halloween, dinner party. Unfortunately, among them are ones that portray witches as old crones. Samantha's mother, Endora (played by Agnes Moorhead), is angered by this and naturally takes her anger out on Darrin by turning him into a werewolf.

The third Halloween episode of *Bewitched*, "Twitch or Treat", centred on a disagreement between Endora and Samantha's Uncle Arthur (played by Paul Lynde) that comes to a head at Endora's Halloween party. It was the show's third Halloween episode in as many years. *Bewitched* would have a Halloween episode the following year as well. In "A Safe and Sane Halloween" Samantha and Darrin's daughter Tabitha (played by Erin Murphy) brings to life a gremlin, a goblin, and Jack O' Lantern from a storybook who then go trick or treating with her. Samantha then has to convince Tabitha to return the characters to the storybook from which they came.

For the first time in its existence *Bewitched* would not have a Halloween episode during the 1968-1969 season. The show would have one last Halloween episode in the 1969-1970 season. The episode once more touches upon the stereotyping of witches, with Endora turning Darrin into a stereotypical old crone. It also includes the trick-or-treat for UNICEF fundraising campaign.

Like *Bewitched*, it should not be surprising that *The Addams Family* featured Halloween episodes given the show centred on a rather macabre family. The first episode, "Halloween with the Addams Family", aired on October 30 1964. In the episode, after their getaway car runs out of gas, two hold-up men take refuge in the Addams Family mansion where the Addamses, quite naturally, are celebrating Halloween. The second episode of *The Addams Family*, "Halloween - Addams Style", aired on October 29 1965. In the episode a neighbour tells little Wednesday (played by Lisa Loring) that there are no real witches or goblins. This upsets Wednesday, so the rest of the family must convince her that witches and goblins are real.

So far I have primarily discussed sitcoms and dramas, but variety shows and music shows sometimes had Halloween editions as well. One of the more famous examples of this was the October 30 1965 edition of *Shindig*. It featured horror legend and guest host Boris Karloff performing "The Peppermint Twist" and "Monster Mash", Ted Cassidy as Lurch from *The Addams Family* performing the novelty song "The Lurch", and various other performers.

In the 1966-1967 season Jackie Gleason revived *The Jackie Gleason Show*. As a result, *The Honeymooners* was also revived. It was on October 29 1966 that one last Halloween sketch of *The Honeymooners* aired. In "The Curse of the Kramdens", Ralph Kramden (played by Jackie Gleason) and Ed Norton (played by Art Carney) have to spend the night in Kramden castle, which is allegedly haunted.

As hard as it might be to believe, the classic science fiction series *Star Trek* also had a Halloween episode. "Catspaw" was written by horror writer Robert Bloch and aired on October 27 1967. It is notable as the first episode filmed featuring Walter Koenig as Ensign Chekov, although it was held back so as to air around Halloween. Other episodes featuring the character then aired before it. "Catspaw" finds the crew of the *Enterprise* encountering witches, a medieval castle, and a sorcerer on a planet. Of course, nothing is as it appears to be.

The sitcom *Nanny and the Professor* had a vaguely supernatural premise, with Juliet Mills playing Nanny, who may or may not have paranormal abilities. In "Nanny and Her Witch's Brew", a classmate's mother becomes convinced Nanny is a witch. The episode aired on November 1 1971. For much of its run *Nanny and the Professor* aired on Friday nights on ABC alongside *The Brady Bunch*. The following year *The Brady Bunch* did its own Halloween episode. In "Fright Night" the Brady boys try scaring the girls with a "ghost". In turn the girls retaliate with their own scare for the boys. "Fright Night" aired on October 27 1972.

For a fairly straight forward sitcom set in the Fifties, it might seem a bit surprising that *Happy Days* has multiple Halloween episodes. The first, "Haunted", aired on October 29 1974. In the episode Richie Cunningham (played by Ron Howard) dismisses his little sister Joanie's (played by Erin Moran) claims that a house is haunted, but then he sees a ghostly figure in a window. The second Halloween episode of *Happy Days* aired a few years later, on October 25 1977. "Fonsillectomy" finds Fonzie (played by Henry Winkler) in the hospital for a tonsillectomy and worried about whom his girlfriend might be with at a Halloween party. The last Halloween episode of *Happy Days*, "Evil Eye", saw Al (played by Al Molinaro) convinced a spell from an old witch with the evil eye has cursed his right arm to do her bidding. It aired on Halloween in 1978.

The police officers on the sitcom *Barney Miller* encountered more than their fair share of unusual characters. In "Werewolf", which aired on October 28 1976, they encountered a man convinced he was a werewolf. As a sitcom it should come as no surprise that *Barney Miller* would have a Halloween episode. What might come as a surprise is that family period drama *The Waltons* did. "The Changeling" aired on October 26 1978. In the episode, as Elizabeth (played by Kami Cotler) nears her 13th birthday, strange things begin to happen, such as a vase moving and then falling to break. The Waltons' cousin Corabeth (played by Ronnie Claire Edwards) suggested that Elizabeth might be haunted by a poltergeist.

The sitcom *The Jefferson*s would part ways with most sitcoms in that it actually did a two part Halloween episode. In part one of "Now You See It, Now You Don't:" it is Halloween and Louise Jefferson (played by Isabel Sanford) witness someone being killed by a man in a rabbit costume. The second part saw Louise confronting the man in the rabbit costume in the Jeffersons' apartment while everyone else was in a bar getting ready for a costume contest. Part One aired on October 21 1979. Part Two aired on October 28 1979.

Most long running shows do a Halloween episode at one point or another. This is no less true of *M*A*S*H*, which did one in its eleventh and final season. "Trick or Treatment" aired on November 1 1962. The episode sees the 4077th celebrating Halloween with their annual party. Unfortunately the party is interrupted by arriving wounded. While working on the wounded the doctors exchange ghost stories.

The Halloween episodes that I've addressed were by no means the only Halloween episodes of shows that aired from the Fifties to the early Eighties. There were yet others, enough that one could probably fill an entire book with them. If anything else, Halloween episodes have perhaps become even more prevalent since the Eighties. While sitcoms have traditionally done at least one Halloween episode during their run, in the past several years shows ranging from *ER* to *NCIS* have done multiple Halloween episodes. The tradition of Halloween episodes that began on radio in the early 20 Century seems to show no signs of slowing on television in the early 21st Century. As long as there are TV shows, it seems likely there will be Halloween episodes.

It's the Great Pumpkin, Charlie Brown

For many people, watching *It's the Great Pumpkin, Charlie Brown* is a Halloween tradition. Over fifty years after its debut it remains popular. There can be no doubt that it is the most popular Halloween TV special of all time.

It's the Great Pumpkin, Charlie Brown debuted on CBS on October 27 1966. It was actually the third of the *Peanuts* specials to air, after *A Charlie Brown Christmas* in 1965 and *Charlie Brown's All-Stars* earlier in 1966. Alongside *A Charlie Brown Christmas* it would arguably become the most popular of the *Peanuts* television specials. Along with *Rudolph the Red-Nosed Reindeer*, *A Charlie Brown Christmas*, and *Frosty the Snowman*, it is one of the very few holiday specials that have aired every single year since the Sixties.

As anyone familiar with the comic strip *Peanuts* knows, the Great Pumpkin is a mythical figure associated with Halloween (not unlike Santa Claus and Christmas) in whom Linus is his only believer. The first reference to the Great Pumpkin was in the *Peanuts* comic strip for October 26 1959, almost exactly seven years before the TV special debuted. In the comic strip Lucy catches Linus writing and asks him what he is doing. Linus informs her that he is writing to the Great Pumpkin and telling him what he wants for Halloween. He goes onto say that the Great Pumpkin loves children and he could see the Great

Pumpkin now rising from the pumpkin patch with his bag of toys. The Great Pumpkin proved to be a rather popular, recurring joke in *Peanuts*, with Linus the only person who believed in him over the years. When it came time to produce a *Peanuts* special for Halloween, it should not have been surprising that the Great Pumpkin would play the central role in its plot.

It's the Great Pumpkin, Charlie Brown would not only be historic as the first time in the *Peanuts* TV specials in which the Great Pumpkin was referenced. It was also historic as the first TV special that portrayed Snoopy's recurring fantasy of fighting the Red Baron, a running joke that had been introduced only a little over a year before the special aired (on October 10 1965).

One of the most memorable comic bits in the special would also enter popular culture--Charlie Brown receiving rocks in his trick-or-treat bag. Charles Schulz had wanted Charlie Brown to receive a rock at one of the houses he visited. Bill Melendez thought it would be better if it happened three times. Executive producer Lee Mendelson didn't approve of the idea at all. Ultimately Lee Mendelson was outvoted and the special portrays Charlie Brown getting a rock in his trick-or-treat bag three times, each time exclaiming, "I got a rock." Viewers were very sympathetic to Charlie's plight. After the special's first airing candy came in from around the world just for Charlie Brown.

It's the Great Pumpkin, Charlie Brown aired on CBS for 34 years. It was in 2001 that ABC got the rights to the *Peanuts* specials. Ever since then it has aired yearly on ABC. Since 2014 ABC has aired the special twice each year.

Given its enormous popularity, it should come as no surprise that *It's the Great Pumpkin, Charlie Brown* is frequently referenced in popular culture. In 2005 the stop motion animation sketch comedy show *Robot Chicken* featured a parody titled "O Great Pumpkin" as part of their episode "Vegetable Funfest". *The Simpsons* also included a parody of the Great Pumpkin, "It's the Grand Pumpkin, Milhouse", as part of their annual "Treehouse of Horror" in 2008. The Great Pumpkin has been referenced in everything from the TV show *Adam-12* to the sitcom *Roseanne* to the horror series *Buffy the Vampire Slayer*.

In an interview Lee Mendelson told the *Washington Post*, "Of the 50 prime-time specials we created with Charles Schulz, I believe *It's the Great Pumpkin, Charlie Brown* is Bill Melendez's animation masterpiece." It would seem that many TV viewers might well agree with him. As mentioned earlier, *It's the Great Pumpkin, Charlie Brown* has aired every single year since its debut in 1966. It was released on VHS and is available on DVD. It seems likely that it will probably still be aired for many years to come.

9 781977 635365